Mindfulness for Borderline Personality Disorder

A Wonderful Journey to Discover Yourself and Release Negative Thoughts

David Paradise

Table of Contents

Introduction

Life with Borderline Personality Disorder is a constant struggle. It can feel as if life is just filled with pain, and there's no reason to stick around anymore. You feel like you just want to call it quits and give up on everything. You desire the sweet release you imagine that death can give you, most days. Other days, what you feel at best is hopeful. You hope something will change. That's about as optimistic as it gets for you.

Well, there is hope. You can set yourself free with the powerful practice of mindfulness. I will be honest with you: It's not going to be easy. You have to deal with all the stuff swirling around in your mind. That is no mean feat because as a sufferer of Borderline Personality Disorder (BPD), it seems like there's no off switch for the chatter that goes on in your mind. You can't just stop thinking. The very best you can hope for is to drown out the noise on the inside with noise on the outside. That's not a very effective stopgap measure, as I'm sure you'll have noticed. When you try to avoid the suffering you go through, science has shown that you only wind up suffering even more. So the answer is definitely not to grow numb to all that you're dealing with.

When Dialectical Behavioral Therapy was developed by Marsha Linehan in 1993, one thing became obvious: At long last, there was a form of treatment that could get results in treating BPD. Those results are chiefly due to the practice of mindfulness. At long last, sufferers of BPD can finally detach from the thoughts and intense feelings, which cause them to suffer.

Besides setting your mind and heart free, mindfulness can help you do better with other coping mechanisms meant to help you deal with pain better. The reason for this is that the whole concept of mindfulness involves teaching you to notice the emotions you feel, without giving away your power by reacting in ways that lead to more suffering. So in this book, we will be focused on understanding mindfulness and help you hone this skill so you can reap the benefits, too.

When you practice mindfulness, over time, all your suffering will evaporate. You may have had to deal with all sorts of treatments before you finally picked up this book on mindfulness, but you must keep an open mind. Once you really dive deep into the practice of mindfulness, you'll begin to notice the beauty around you, which you were blind to in the past. You'll notice that you're not as anxious or as depressed as you used to be. Your relationships will improve because of it, and you'll find that you quite like being alive, because you actually do **feel alive** again.

Chapter One: The DSM of Borderline Personality Disorder

If you're a sufferer of Borderline Personality Disorder, then you don't need a dictionary or expert to tell you what it is you have to go through every day. This is your life: Constantly swinging from one end to the other because of your intense emotions; constantly dealing with conflict in the relationships which matter to you the most; constantly loathing yourself, especially because you can't seem to get a handle on your anger which pushes those near and dear to you away; ever afraid that sooner or later, everyone will leave you, no matter what they do or say to reassure you that that's not the case; struggling with feelings of suicide, because you think at least if you're dead then all the pain and suffering you're going through an end at long last.

It may seem like a hopeless case, but believe me, it isn't. There are lots of people living with BPD who continue to improve day after day. All you need is the correct treatment, and in a matter of time, you'll find your life is a lot more rewarding. There's no reason you can't beat this. You can, and you will, just like all the others who have. You are never alone.

The Stats

In the United States of America alone, 1.6% of the population suffers from BPD. It may seem like nothing, but 1.6% actually comes to about 4 million people. Sadly, BPD is not quite as known as other illnesses out there.

When it comes to gender, studies have shown that women are more likely to have BPD than men. At any time, only 25% of those diagnosed with this disorder are men. This means for every four people with BPD; three will be women. It's still not quite clear why there's a higher tendency for women to suffer from BPD than men. At the moment, the theories floating around are that women are more likely to seek treatment than men, or that during diagnosis there is some gender bias at play (such as men with BPD being misdiagnosed with other conditions like PTSD), or that women are simply more likely to have BPD.

As for the figures on suicide, 70% of BPD sufferers will attempt to take their own lives at least once. 8 to 10 percent will actually follow through with suicide. This percentage of BPD sufferers actually accounts for over 50 times the suicide rate in the whole population. It's unclear why this is the case; the working theories are that BPD sufferers do not have a clue where to go for treatment, or they get misdiagnosed and so are not given the proper treatment.

While the population of BPD sufferers in America is pegged at 1.6%, it could actually be a lot higher than that. According to a recently conducted study, at least 40% of BPD sufferers had been misdiagnosed with other mental health disorders, such as borderline disorder, among others. The reason this happens is that the public and the healthcare system is better informed on those other disorders, which happen to be a lot easier to treat with the right medication, compared to Borderline Personality Disorder.

Yet another factor that can cause misdiagnosis is that sufferers may have comorbidities along with BPD itself. It's not an uncommon phenomenon. Up to 20% of BPD sufferers have also been found to suffer from bipolar disorder. On account of this, diagnosis and treatment are even trickier than usual.

On the whole, studies have established that the prognosis for BPD is not nearly as detrimental as it was once believed to be. According to research, about half of those who have been diagnosed with Borderline Personality Disorder will eventually no longer fit the diagnosis after about two years. In a decade's time, a whopping 88% of those who suffered from BPD will no longer have the symptoms. Now, this doesn't mean that BPD is not a serious illness, or that it should not be given the attention it deserves. I merely point out the stats to help you see that you are not a lost cause. This disorder is not going to have you behind bars for life. You'll see that as you continue to read this book.

Borderline Personality Disorder Defined

Over the years, the criteria by which Borderline Personality Disorder was defined have morphed. So as we attempt to define BPD, we're going to do so in such a way that the current definition we come up with will still be relevant in the future.

First, we begin with the Diagnostic and Statistical Manual of Mental Disorders, or DSM, for short. This is a publication of the American Psychiatric Association and is the leading authority on all information pertaining to psychiatric disorders. It provides a comprehensive list of symptoms for each disorder and also makes it clear what the quantity and severity of the symptoms need to be, before concluding on a certain diagnosis.

For BPD, it is required that there be at least five of the following symptoms:

• A trail of interpersonal relationships that are unstable and continue to ricochet between idealization, devaluation, and splitting.

- Constant efforts to prevent feelings of abandonment, whether real or imagined.

- A perpetually shaky sense of identity

- Continuous, impulsive, self-damaging behavior, especially when it comes to finances, sex, drugs, daredevil stunts, dietary choices, and so on.

- Consistent suicidal thoughts and behavior, including threats, and self-harm

- Instability of emotions on a daily basis, which includes intense sadness, anxiety, or general irritability lasting for a matter of hours, and on rare occasions, some days

- A persistent feeling of emptiness

- A complete lack of control when it comes to anger, and temper, which could be the cause of consistent, violent physical fights

- Paranoid ideation on account of stress, which is usually transient, in addition to serious symptoms of dissociation

The trouble with the DSM requiring at least 5 of these symptoms is that there are at least 256 different combinations of said symptoms. In other words, each person out of 256 BPD sufferers could possibly have a unique series of symptoms. It's rare to find conditions that have symptoms with so many different permutations.

Now, in order to get a better handle on Borderline Personality Disorder, let's go through each symptom.

Efforts to Prevent Feelings of Abandonment

As a sufferer of BPD, you might find that you have a very intense, sometimes irrational fear that the people who are near and dear to you will one day walk out of your life for good. On the one hand, you'd do whatever you can to not be alone, so you actively seek out relationships. On the other hand, once you're in a relationship, you become consumed with the fear of being abandoned by them, and as such, you begin to act clingy and dependent. Naturally, being clingy is not an attractive trait, and this repulses the other person enough to create distance between you both. So you worry that all that needs to happen is just one more goof, and they're gone for good. Because you're scared, you might find yourself self-harming, which could be beyond the ability of your partner or friend to deal with. So they leave, and you find someone new, and it all begins afresh.

It doesn't take much to make you fear being abandoned. All you need is something you perceive as rejection, even if it really isn't that big a deal. It could be that your loved one cancels on your plans to go skiing together, or your doctor is running just a little late for an appointment you both had. That could be all it takes to make you feel fear. It doesn't matter what your loved one canceled because he had to deal with a work emergency, or that the doctor is trying desperately hard to save someone who's about to die. You become intensely angry because to you it seems that you don't matter. Other people can see that the rage you're displaying is a little too much for the current circumstance, but you don't care.

When the feeling of abandonment overcomes you, you do anything you can to feel reassured that you're okay and that no one is going to leave you anytime soon. One of these reassurance-seeking actions could involve incessantly calling your loved one or your friend, just so they can comfort you and quell your fears. The trouble is you call so much that they get irritated by you. Over the course of time, your behavior leads to the end of the relationships and friendships you have.

Extremely Intense and Highly Unstable Interpersonal Relationships

Along with the fear of being abandoned, you also have a fear of being all alone. Because of this fear, BPD sufferers find it incredibly easy to become attached to others in all their relationships. This attachment is very intense and often happens incredibly fast. You may recognize this feeling of attachment when it becomes absolutely imperative that you get to know whether or not the other person feels the same way you do. You need to know that what they feel for you is just as deep as what you feel for them. You find comfort in knowing that you're loved as deeply as you love and that when you're in pain, the other person suffers as though it were their own pain, too.

So when people who do not have BPD do not respond the way you'd like them to — since they do not feel what you feel as deeply as you do — you feel hurt. The pain you feel gets to a point where you might begin saying really hurtful things you don't necessarily mean, just in a bid to make them feel the pain you feel too. More often than not, when the words leave your mouth, you are overwhelmed with shame and regret. It's not uncommon to find you swinging from being demeaning to idealizing the same person you just hurt. As for the object of your affection, it becomes difficult for them to deal with you, since you're anything but predictable. They become overwhelmed with your antics, and eventually, they might end up doing the very thing you were afraid they would do. They leave.

A Shaky Sense of Identity

You might find that it's incredibly difficult for you to know yourself. You don't quite know who you really are. Your values change with the wind. One second you were extremely passionate about certain goals, romantic inclinations, interests, and values; the next, you've done a complete 180, and you're just as passionate about the complete opposite of everything you hold near and dear not too long ago. Because of these sudden changes, you find that you're the exact antithesis of stability, whether it's about work, love, or your passions. This causes complete chaos in your relationships with others, and you are all the more unpredictable for it. Other people find they cannot rely on you and have to walk on eggshells when you're around.

Impulsiveness

Being excessively impulsive is your forte, it seems. On account of this, you wind up in trouble more often than not. You act without thinking about what the consequences might be to yourself and to the people around you. Sometimes, you **are** indeed aware of the consequences, but you deliberately ignore them.

Usually, when you're impulsive, you're also drowning in really intense emotions, which could be brought on by the fact that you're dealing with a lot of issues in your relationships. There are all sorts of ways that BPD sufferers can act impulsively;

however, the ways that pose the most danger to yourself and others often involve drug abuse, self-harm, reckless sex, and careless driving. These actions are not necessarily suicidal in and of themselves, but they are no less dangerous and can have a major impact on your health and wellbeing in the long run.

Consistent Self-Harming and Suicidal Behavior

While suicide and self-harm are two separate concepts, they can often be lumped together, because studies have shown that those who self-harm are 30% more likely to commit suicide than the rest of the population. The risk is even higher for women who engage in self-harming behaviors than it is for men. The rate for suicide goes up within a period of six months, after the very first occurrence of self-injury. The point I'd like to make here is that while self-harm and suicide serve different causes, in the end, they share a lot more than you'd think.

As with being impulsive, self-harming is one of the major reasons that BPD sufferers go for therapy. The reason you engage in self-harm is that you find it helps you deal with your emotions. You find it oddly soothing when you engage in such behavior as cutting. Other reasons for engaging in self-harm include the need to feel alive and less numb. The physical pain from cutting themselves helps them deal with the deeper, underlying emotional pain, which drives the behavior. While you may view cutting as an efficient solution, this can be pretty problematic, not just for you but for the people in your life, as well. They become extremely worried about you, and you know this. So you do your best to keep your cutting a secret. You know it's not a great solution for the long haul, but you do it anyway.

On account of the rollercoaster of emotions you feel, which makes your life feel like a living nightmare, you start to think it would just be better if you could put an end to everything. You wake up each morning dismayed at the fact that you're still alive, still breathing. You begin to fantasize about all the different ways you could possibly die. Sure, in the beginning, they are only thoughts. However, these thoughts can be stubborn and come upon you in a forceful torrent that you just cannot buck no matter how hard you try. Eventually, you give in. You find yourself actively strategizing, so you can come up with the perfect way to take a bow and exit stage left from the play of life. Before you know it, you've made an actual attempt to take your life.

The stats on suicide and BPD show that in every 10 cases of BPD, which have led to hospitalization, at least nine will have attempted suicide, while the remaining one will have completed suicide. The implication of this is that when it comes to BPD, most of the suicide attempts result in failures. As a result, the survivors feel like they've been cheated from getting a chance at freedom, or they feel overcome with shame at not being able to see it through to the end. They also have to deal with the fact that for the most part, society will accuse them of just being "attention-seekers" or put them down for self-harming, saying it's nothing but a cry for help. However, science has shown that people self-harm and commit suicide for reasons other than the simple need for attention.

Emotional Volatility

As a sufferer of BPD, you have to deal with mood instability all the time. You're up right now, and in a few hours, you're down. Yes, this happens to people who don't have BPD, but the difference is when it comes to you, the sufferer, the swings are wilder, and more often than not they are caused by the conflicts you experience in your interpersonal relationships, as well as the frustration you feel with yourself. Also, you feel things more deeply than others do, and for even longer. It takes you a lot longer than the average person to revert to feeling okay again.

Yet another thing that happens is when you feel emotion powerfully, you genuinely believe you've always felt the way you do. When you're feeling ecstatic, that's okay, somewhat. However, when you're feeling down in the dumps, it makes it hard to remember that there were times you were actually happy, and so it feels as though you are doomed to feel this way forever, further aggravating the feelings of suicide that you feel. It doesn't matter that you felt amazing as recently as yesterday; you just can't see your way through the dark cloud hovering over you. When people try to tell you you're not going to feel this way forever, you find yourself even more irritated, irate and misunderstood on top of everything else.

Constant Feeling of Emptiness

Most people with BPD often struggle with feelings of emptiness. You may feel the emptiness come on strong whenever you're left all alone. The emptiness within makes it incredibly difficult for you to set goals for yourself, or to aspire to anything. On account of your complete lack of aspirations, others judge you harshly, saying that you simply don't care about anything, or that you lack the basic motivation to move forward in life.

You'll find more often than not when you're with other people; you don't feel quite as empty as when you're all alone. That being said, there's also the problem that arises where others find they are unable to give you the level of closeness or intimacy you're seeking. As a result, you've got to walk that fine line between being close to them, and being the clingy one. This is no walk in the park.

Intense Rage and Anger

With BPD, it's like every little thing can set you off. You just want to call it quits, but you know that you can't, and so that just causes your frustration to build, until it's no longer frustration but pure, unbridled rage. You're angry at everyone in your life for the most inconsequential of things. You're angry even when you hear that the people you love have moved up and ahead in life because that implies they've all gone ahead and left you behind. You want nothing more than to scream your head off and break everything you can around you.

Does your anger seem a tad excessive to others? Yes, it definitely is. They think you're blowing things way out of proportion, and you need to take a chill pill. When they tell you this, you only get even more outraged, and this drives a wedge between you and the people who matter to you in your life.

It's not hard to see the way these symptoms are all interconnected with one another. No one likes to have to deal with angry people, and so because of that, they avoid being with you. Since they avoid dealing with you, this triggers in you the fear that you're going to be abandoned by them. So you begin to act out by becoming excessively clingy, and when your advances are rejected, you want to hurt them back, so you lash out by saying things you don't mean. Next thing you know, they're gone for good.

Dissociative and Paranoid Symptoms

These are the norm when it comes to BPD, especially when you're going through a lot of stress. Even if it's not the case, you get it into your head that the people in your life are doing their best to make you feel like crap, hurt you, and generally make your life a living hell. You feel like you're not really existing, or like it's the world itself, which does not actually exist. You have a weird disconnect from yourself, where it looks like you're just an observer watching your body as it goes through the motions of living from day to day. This is even more common with BPD sufferers who were abused in their childhood or who went through some sort of trauma at some point in life.

Chapter Two: Putting The Pieces Together

We're going to put together an integrated and comprehensive definition of Borderline Personality Disorder, but before we do that, I am going to cover a few other symptoms, which are not already listed in the DSM.

Other BPD Symptoms Missing From the DSM

While the DSM gives a comprehensive list of symptoms associated with BPD, there are a few other symptoms that are not listed in it. You may or may not experience these additional symptoms, but chances are you'll find them very familiar.

Feeling Perpetually Misunderstood

It may seem to you that no matter what you do, no one ever gets you. No one truly understands what drives you to do what you do. This misunderstanding is often on account of how extreme your behavior and feelings are. Most people cannot relate to that level of intensity. When you don't feel understood, you also feel like you're all by yourself in the world. If this were something you have experienced or are still experiencing, then you would find group therapy to be of immense benefit to you. Group therapy will help you realize you're not alone, that there are others just like you who understand exactly what you're going through.

Self-Loathing

This symptom is quite a dangerous, disturbing one. You always find something to hate about yourself. You struggle with feelings of low self-worth, thinking you're the worst person on the planet and that you always ruin things, no matter what. You blame and castigate yourself for all sorts of things — including stuff that really wasn't your fault, or might have had nothing to do with you. If you notice any positive thing in your life at all, you do your best to quash it and dismiss it. You assume that you are just the most toxic being on earth. You think you are evil incarnate. Being plagued with thoughts such as these, it's not hard to see how you would come to hate yourself passionately.

Oversensitivity to Other's Emotions

People with BPD tend to be extremely sensitive to other people's emotions. If you notice someone around you is anxious, then you get nervous. If they're angry, then you're angry too. If they're sad, you feel just as sad. You might also find it odd that for some reason, other people do not pick up on the emotions swirling around them as easily as you do. You may have freaked out some of your friends and family by being able to tell how they feel even before they figure out their own feelings. If the people around you are not self-aware, this ability of yours could be even more bothersome.

This might sound like a neat superpower to people who don't have BPD, but it's not that way at all. This ability you have gets you into trouble more often than not, because when you sense someone you care about is annoyed about something, you take that on, assuming that you're the one at fault. Next thing you know, you're overcome with the fear of abandonment again. Or you could sense that your friend is very happy about something, and rather than see it as just that; you could assume that it's the love they're feeling for you when that's not the case.

Choosing to Be Right, No Matter the Cost

As humans, we're usually able to tell right from wrong, and we're proud of that fact. This is why when it's time to make critical decisions, most of us choose to do the "right" thing, which depends on our values, morals, and faith, among other factors. As someone who has BPD, you get the sense that life hasn't dealt you a good hand. For this reason, you find yourself holding on to your stance on some issue vehemently, even if you are clearly causing a lot of grief for the people around you. You don't care that your refusal to let go of the need to be right is ruining the already tenuous relationships you have with the people you care about.

Losing All Sense of Time

Not everyone who has BPD experiences this symptom; however, it's not uncommon. You find it hard to keep a continuous sense of time, which makes sense. To you, it's like life is just an endless loop. You're stuck on repeat, constantly recycling your emotions, unable to tell the difference from one circumstance to another. You start to feel that the concept of time does not exist and that this is an eternity. You're stuck, and you're never going to escape your life no matter what.

Another way you lose a sense of time could be that you get over traumatic or sad experiences really quickly. Say you were in a relationship that lasted for many years. You could get over it in a matter of days, as though nothing ever happened, or none of it ever mattered to you. This is how you're able to deal with the pain that comes from relationships ending. When people try to get you to deal with your grief, what happens instead is you dig your heels in, insisting that you have always felt the way you do. Any memory of feeling differently seems to have been completely erased from your mind.

As you lose all sense of time, you'll find yourself interweaving all the trauma you have experienced in the past into the present as well. Next thing you know, you feel like you're in pieces and empty. You never feel like you're whole, or like there's anything of substance to you. You don't remember things in a linear fashion. Memories from decades ago can leap out at you, and it would feel as though it was literally seconds ago that you lived through the memory.

The Need for Perfection

When you need to take action, you can sometimes find yourself paralyzed by the need to do it all perfectly. The thing is that there is no such thing as perfection, and your choice to achieve perfection is a battle you're never going to win. You'll find that your need for perfection will keep you from doing the things you really need to do. You are terrified of doing anything less than perfect, and so you never bother to start anyway. After all, you can't muck it up if you never even do it in the first place.

You might find yourself a little too obsessed with the details. You constantly sweat the small stuff. Since you need to get it just right, you become unreasonable and incredibly rigid about things. You might find yourself constantly restarting projects, and in the end, it's never done. You find that on account of your need for perfection, you feel so overwhelmed by all the work that you've got to do.

Seeming Manipulative

More often than not, the people in your life would describe you as incredibly manipulative. This is yet another huge reason many people dealing with BPD come in for therapy. When queried about how you came to the conclusion that you are manipulative, your answer is something along the lines of, "Everyone tells me I am!"

The people in your life feel like you're always trying to put one over them. They feel like you're always lying and looking for ways to control them. In your mind, though, that's not what you intended. You never meant to be seen that way. You never set out to deceive your loved ones, or control them.

All that's happening here is you're doing what you think is your best. You're harming yourself because it's the only way you know to deal with pain, not because you're trying to upset others or make them feel guilty for not being there as much as you'd like or something. While this is the case, no matter what you say, it will seem to others like the whole point behind all you do is to manipulate them so you can have your way.

The thing to keep in mind, though, is that someone calling you manipulative does not automatically mean that you are. It's simply their interpretation of your actions.

Putting It All Together

The best way for us to achieve this is to make use of the system of Dysregulation, which is an approach by Marsha Linehann in which we organize all the symptoms into five specific areas of difficulty, which the BPD patient has to deal with. Let's take a look at them.

Interpersonal Dysregulation

Interpersonal Dysregulation means you've got a lot of turbulence in all your relationships. You don't find it easy to sustain your relationships, and you're in constant fear that everyone will leave you eventually.

Emotion Dysregulation

Emotion Dysregulation is simply the inability to manage your emotions in a way that is healthy. You find that you are unable to deal with the intense wave of emotions that you seem always to be drowning in. You find that your emotions are extremely dynamic, and more often than not, they are buffeted about by the winds of the conflicts you deal with in your interpersonal relationships. Also, as part of emotion Dysregulation, you find it hard to pinpoint the exact emotions you're dealing with at each point in time.

Behavioral Dysregulation

Behavioral Dysregulation implies the use of dangerous behaviors to deal with your emotions. You find yourself indulging in reckless, unsafe sex, reckless driving, self-injurious behaviors, terrible dieting, drug abuse, and other things that could end your life and put others at risk as well.

Self-Dysregulation

What self-Dysregulation implies is that you cannot see yourself as a whole human being. You struggle with your sense of self-identity. Your values, morals, interests, and passions are constantly changing. On account of this, you find yourself easily bored, dealing with feelings of loneliness, and overcome by emptiness.

Cognitive Dysregulation

Cognitive Dysregulation implies you're constantly losing touch with yourself. You become dissociated from reality, assuming that none of what you experience is real, or that the people you know and the experiences you've gone through are not real. You could also assume you are the one who is the only unreal thing, as you simply observe the world around you passively. You might find yourself dealing with paranoia sometimes, always assuming that people are out to get you.

When You Can't Manage Your Emotions

Dealing with BPD, you might find it incredibly draining not to give in to the whirlwind of emotions you feel. It's not like you deliberately want to explode. It's that you **just can't help yourself.** The ability to regulate your emotions is a skill that most people have honed over time. They take it for granted, though.

Many people assume that you are very capable of getting a lid on your emotions, but you're choosing to be difficult about it. They don't realize how hard you really are trying. If they could show a bit more compassion towards you, and stow the judgment, then it would be an even easier go of things for you as you learn to be better at handling your emotions.

Let's Talk About Habits

As you already know, a habit is something you do consistently, without even being aware of it. As humans, we are creatures of habit. We're used to repetition. It can be useful, as this is the way you pick up useful life skills like learning to drive properly or eating food you need to survive. For the most part, you are unaware of your habits, unless you decide to pay a little more attention to the things you do and the way you do them.

Habits are useful because when it comes to essential life skills, you never need to overthink the process. You just do what you would do, and that makes you more efficient with your time and energy. The habits have become ingrained, an inseparable part of your neurological wiring. However, this can be a bad thing when we're talking about bad habits that we desperately need to break, especially in light of BPD.

How Habits Become Habits

The way to develop a habit is through repetition, plain and simple. Each time you repeat something, a whole bunch of nerve cells is fired, and that creates and strengthens neural connections connected to the action you're repeating, making it easier over time. When you're working out, for instance, in the beginning, it's not easy at all. However, the more reps you do, the more your muscles remember, and the stronger they get. The stronger they get, the easier your workouts become.

Similarly, you can train yourself to learn certain behaviors and do them on autopilot — even if the action is detrimental to you.

Bad Habits

In the context of BPD, constantly engaging in self-harming behaviors leads to more self-harming. If you indulge in cutting, then you're going to indulge in more cutting. If you're constantly thinking suicidal thoughts, then you'll be thinking even more of the same. If you're constantly entertaining self-loathing thoughts, then you'll be engaging in more of the same. And even worse, *you'll be getting better and better at these bad habits, each time.*

Your brain does not have the ability to tell the difference between what's good for you and what isn't when it comes to habits. The mechanism is the same, whether it's a good thing you're training yourself to be better at or a terrible thing. All your brain understands is that you keep repeating this action over and over, and so it must be pretty important to learn. So it helps you get better at whatever it is, good or bad. Say you decide you like cutting since it helps you get a better grip on your emotions.

Other people may think it's a terrible idea, but for you, it's not. You've found this to be the most effective way to handle your feelings. Your brain is aware that you need to learn this, and that becomes a habit. The only way to break it is to become aware of when you're indulging in it, and then understand the triggers behind your choice to cut. This is where mindfulness can be of immense benefit to you. Mindfulness can and will serve you in the long run. It's effective behavior versus ineffective behavior like self-harm.

Certainty versus Curiosity

Sometimes it feels like you know 100% what the other person is thinking about, or what their motivations are. You feel so sure that you're not even willing to consider you could be wrong. Rather than continue to maintain your certainty, consider adopting a curious stand instead. What I mean is that it would make your life that much better if you simply assume that you could be wrong about people's intentions. Become curious about what it is that really drives others: more curiosity and less certainty.

The reason I advise you to be more curious and less certain is that when you buy into your preconceived notions about people not liking you, you cause yourself needless suffering since your assumption is based on a false premise. In other words, you'd be swallowing painkillers for a headache that isn't yours and doesn't even exist, to begin with.

Everything or Nothing at All

Nearly everyone experiences some degree of cognitive distortion, meaning there are times when our minds are completely sold on the idea that fiction is fact. We convince ourselves that the irrational is rational. When you've got BPD, this could be a serious problem, as you'd be in for a world of hurt. Some of the ways you can find yourself dealing with cognitive distortion include:

• **Thinking in Black-and-white.** For you, there are no shades of grey. It's either one thing or the other. You just can't see how, in certain situations, the lines can be blurred.

• **Personalizing.** As far as you're concerned, every single thing that people do or say is about you.

• **Filtering.** This is when you choose to ignore anything that's good and focus only on the bad stuff. So you've got your mind programmed to sift through all the input you receive so that only the things that support your negative outlook can filter through to you.

• **Creating catastrophes out of thin air.** This is constantly imagining that something bad is going to happen, despite evidence to the contrary. You believe the worst will happen on account of the most trivial issues, which may come up.

• **Overgeneralizing.** You take one occurrence and based on that, you make broad, sweeping generalizations about everything else, disregarding logic or evidence to the contrary.

• **Believing in absolute shoulds.** You are firmly convinced that things *should* always play out in a certain way. You believe people *should* act in this way or that way. You then get outraged when things don't go the way you believe they "should."

• **Rigidly believing in fairness.** You believe you know what is fair and what isn't. It irks you to no end when people don't see eye to eye with you on the issue of fairness, and you dig your heels in even further.

Now that you have a clear idea of what Borderline Personality Disorder entails, and you know the symptoms according to the DSM, as well as those not listed therein, you are in a better position to identify whether you or a loved one may be suffering from BPD. The symptoms are nothing to sneeze at, as in so many ways, they can affect the quality of your life adversely.

In this book, you and I will go on a journey, exploring what mindfulness is, and how the practice of it can help you in addition to whatever therapeutic measures you're working with at the moment. That said, let's move on to the next chapter, where we'll discuss mindfulness in detail, and you'll learn how to use the practice of mindfulness to ease your pain and suffering from BPD.

Chapter Three: Mindfulness

When it comes to Dialectical Behavior Therapy (DBT), mindfulness plays a central role. We're going to take a look at the practice of mindfulness, and see how you can use it to help you ameliorate the symptoms of Borderline Personality Disorder so that you can finally take charge of your life.

Mindfulness is a unique practice, nowhere near similar to anything you've done before. While it may not be familiar to you, you must keep our mind open, because the benefits you will receive from this practice are definitely worth it. Countless others who suffered from BPD as you do have found mindfulness to be a great help to them.

Before we dive into mindfulness, we're going to explore why mindfulness is so important in dealing with BPD. This exploration is necessary so that you can understand why and how it works, and be even more encouraged to stick with your practice.

What Is Mindfulness

Mindfulness is all about deliberately paying attention, being in the moment, observant, without passing any judgment on what is observed. Mindfulness is so important. It's something you can achieve through consistent practice. In short, mindfulness is more than a practice. It's a lifestyle.

Mindfulness is all about being fully grounded in the present. You're fully aware of everything that's happening, both within you and outside of you. When you practice mindfulness, the only place is here, and the only time is now.

It's not about being some Buddhist monk. You could be completely grounded in the present moment as you sip a cup of coffee, or as you read a book, or take a walk. It's really all about giving your full attention to the present moment while keeping your mind open. You won't be making any judgment calls or forming any opinions about what you observe at the moment. You remain open and accepting of what is, without needing to change it or control it in some way. In mindfulness, you focus your attention on the task at hand, whether it's your breathing, or reading a book. When your mind wanders — and it will — you simply bring it back to the moment. It's okay if you get distracted. Thoughts, emotions, and the stuff happening around you can all vie for your attention. However, when you notice you've gone off track, all you have to do is return your attention to the moment.

The Origin of Mindfulness

Mindfulness as a practice is something that has existed for thousands of years. While it's primarily attributed to Eastern religious philosophies, as you comb through history, you'll find that all around the world mindfulness as a practice has always existed in some form or the other, whether it's the Hindu's yogic meditation, the Jewish kabbalah meditations, or the Islamic Sufi meditations. The common thread you'll find through all of these different methods of practicing mindfulness is that there is a need to focus your attention. It could be on the concept of love, a mantra, God, gratitude, the breath, or the heart. Whatever you're focused on, the point is to keep your attention on it. None of this means you need to adopt some religion to reap the rewards of mindfulness. However, it would be helpful to pay some attention to the Eastern origins of mindfulness, as the Buddhist way of thinking has a lot of philosophies that work perfectly for the soul suffering from BPD.

Before science became what we know it to be today, the only way people could really understand the world around them was by observation and contemplation. Through this, the Buddhists realized millennia ago that humans are dynamic in nature. We're never stuck as the same person for the rest of our lives. "Buddha" is Sanskrit for "to awaken "and "to know." The Buddhist philosophy is basically that once we awaken to the truth of our dynamic nature, once we accept the roles our bodies, minds, and emotions play in changing us from one state to another, then we will finally be able to do away with the misery of feeling that everything is set in stone.

This is very useful knowledge because, as most BPD sufferers will tell you, they often feel without a doubt that things are permanent. Nothing ever changes. It's all static. They are able to rationalize all this with their emotions backing them up. As a result, the BPD patient finds it difficult to fully enjoy life and soak up every experience it has to offer. You might find that more often than not, you have chosen not to be curious about life. You've chosen to ignore what is going on in the moment, more often than not.

The etymology of the word "mindfulness" is based in Pali, which is the language used in Buddhist psychology. Mindfulness is drawn from the word *sati*, which basically involves giving people all the help they need to understand all that they experience on a deeper level, and ultimately help free them from the suffering that they contend with every day.

The practice of mindfulness is rooted in the basic philosophy of "The Four Noble Truths."

The Buddhist's Four Noble Truths

Whether we're talking about Vajrayana, Theravada, or Zen, there are Four Noble Truths, which are woven seamlessly into every Buddhist tradition that exists. These truths tackle suffering head-on and emphasize the need to become still. It's important to keep these concepts in your mind because as we move along, you'll find yourself resonating with them.

The reason these truths are called "noble" is that you'll find your level of awareness will naturally rise, on account of them. You'll be able to cut through the seemingly automatic nature of your actions and reactions so that you can finally understand your hidden motivations. You'll become truly and fully aware — and that is the goal of this book.

In the Western part of the world, by default, we think of suffering as a terrible thing. We believe we must do all we can to avoid it, or end it as swiftly as possible. As a sufferer of BPD, this need to avoid suffering is felt even more acutely than non-sufferers. In fact, you can probably agree that you spend the bulk of your life running away from people and circumstances you suspect will cause you to feel pain or to suffer. You run so hard that when you really get right down to it, you will never find the peace and freedom you seek. While the West is all about avoiding suffering, the Buddhists take an entirely different stance on the whole concept. Let's see how.

Noble Truth Number One: *Dukkha*. Life means suffering. I know, for the most part, a lot of people would agree with this statement. One way or another, all humans have suffered in varying degrees. More often than not, the suffering is beyond bearable. It feels unjust, and we all want nothing more than for it to end. This noble truth is an acceptance that the entirely of life is about suffering, physically, psychologically, and emotionally.

The best way to deal with ***dukkha*** is to be okay with the fact that all things in life are transient. It's going to be a tough pill to swallow if you hold on to the black-and-white way of thinking of things. Once you accept this, however, you'll find your life becomes full of the exact opposite of suffering. You'll find peace and joy in everything. You'll be a lot calmer. You simply need to accept that all things — good, bad, or neutral — are transient. Simply be with the moment.

Noble Truth Number Two: *Samudaya.* **All suffering is caused by attachment.** When you vehemently hold onto as much as you can in life because you're afraid of losing it all, you **do** end up losing it all, and then you suffer for it. Also, when you hold onto the past — past grievances, betrayals, hurts, experiences, and beliefs — you'll find that you only suffer for it.

Recall we've already pointed out the fact that life is truly dynamic in nature. This means nothing is the same. The past can never be the same as the present, nor will the present be the same as the future. You only inflict suffering on yourself if you choose to hold on so tightly to it all. But that's what is prevalent in the West. We've become so unaware of the fact that we are clinging to our past. For those with BPD, this causes even more pain than for others. Sadly, if you've got BPD, then chances are you will cling on to the past even harder and longer than the average person, and this just fills your heart with endless and needless pain.

When you expect people to act as they always have, or to think of you as they've always done, you're asking for a world of hurt. Even if you somehow manage to get every person and thing to conform to your past ideals, this does not necessarily mean you'll find true happiness. Also, that can be an incredibly frustrating way to live, trying to control things, so they reflect your ideals just so.

When you don't understand that change is unstoppable and ever constant, you'll find yourself suffering, because you are unable to accept the present moment as it is. You

Noble Truth Number Three: *Nirodha*. It is possible to end suffering. Once you have acknowledged the fact that suffering is inevitable, and that it's caused by needless attachments, then you can move on to the third truth, which is that you **can** end your suffering. You really can find the joy, freedom, and peace of mind that you have sought for so long.

Now that you have become aware, you'll find it easier to let go of all the attachments you have been clinging onto all this time. Once you do this, you will find yourself living a very mindful, very present life. As a result, you are able to truly and fully enjoy your life.

I will grant you that at this point, this could be a rather difficult idea to accept, but just know that all you need is to be mindful. Doubts will flood your mind. This is natural. Mindfulness is not a walk in the park. You've got to practice to get better, just like with any other skill. Just keep in mind that you can become adept at mindfulness, once you feel the doubt flooding your mind. In fact, I appreciate the doubt. Use your doubts to help you stay in the present. See them with no judgment. Do not pronounce judgment on your doubts, or on yourself for having them. Watch them and let them go.

Noble Truth Number Four: *Magga.* **There is a way to end your suffering.** There is a path out of the suffering that plagues you. That path is mindfulness itself. To begin down this path, you must become aware of your emotions. You must become aware of the thoughts that float through your mind, as well as your actions. Then you must go a step further by showing yourself compassion, extending that same compassion to others, through the practice of mindfulness. The further you walk down this path, the more you'll find your suffering and pain fading away into nothingness. You'll no longer crave the things you should let go of. You'll finally have set yourself free.

Merging East and West

In recent times, the West has become aware of the benefits that the Eastern practice of mindfulness has to offer, physically and mentally. In the US today, it's not uncommon to find the practice being implemented in offices, schools, hospices, and other places. Thanks to modern science, the benefits of mindfulness are becoming even more obvious, and the practice is now deemed important enough to be studied. Thousands of studies have been conducted on mindfulness, and it looks like thousands more will happen.

Among the benefits modern-day science has discovered, mindfulness is amazing for relieving stress. Today's world has a lot more stressors than ever before, and mindfulness is one of the best, most wholesome ways to stay sane in a world too loud and too bright. It's also been discovered that mindfulness eases the symptoms of disorders like anxiety and panic — including panic caused by agoraphobia (the fear of people). Mindfulness helps you become more positive and feel better about yourself. It also helps you keep a handle on your emotions. The practice is of immense benefit to sufferers of depression, people who struggle with binge eating, and those who are dealing with Post-Traumatic Stress Disorder (PTSD), especially when it comes to the tendency of PTSD sufferers to enact numbing and avoiding behaviors, on account of sexual abuse they experienced as children.

When it comes to BPD, studies have shown that practicing mindfulness is more than enough to help you conquer the symptoms, which you struggle with. The more mindful you become, the more your mood improves overall. You'll find you're less impulsive, more present, and more attentive to yourself, others, and the moment. Mindfulness even helps you handle anything you'd find distressing a lot better than usual. With constant practice, you'll find that you're less angry and less likely to lash out at people. Because of the amazing benefits you can get from mindfulness, it's a part of Dialectical Behavioral Therapy, and there's also Mindfulness-Based Cognitive Therapy, which is just as beneficial as well.

The Difference between Meditation and Mindfulness

Now you understand what mindfulness is about, and you know of its origins. You also know that it's become widely accepted in the West, especially as a treatment modality in the mental health space. The more you dive into the subject, the more new things you'll learn. With that in mind, it is imperative that we make clear the difference between mindfulness and meditation because meditation is something you will encounter quite often when exploring mindfulness.

More often than not, people use the terms "meditation" and "mindfulness" interchangeably. However, others assume there is a difference between the two concepts. Talk about meditation, and what comes to mind is monks in a monastery. As far as this book is concerned, meditation is a path to mindfulness.

In order to meditate, you must consider your sessions as serious as business appointments with yourself. What I mean by that is you must make time every day to sit in silence, and you must show up. You have no options. You must sit for the same amount of time, and it would help if you had a dedicated space for meditating. This is not a prerequisite, as you'll find the longer you stick with it, the easier it is for you to slip into the meditative state wherever, whenever.

Meditation is not the only way you can practice mindfulness. You can be mindful as you go about your day-to-day activities, but that is not meditation. Whatever route you go, the whole point is to increase your level of awareness and presence in your life.

Chapter Four: The BPD Brain versus the Mindful Brain

If you want the best out of your mindfulness practice, then it is worth exploring the neurobiological differences between the brain plagued by BPD, and the mindful brain. The reason you do the things you do and think and feel as you do is all in your head. All emotions are a result of brain activity, and so we need to peek beneath the hood to understand what causes your pain, suffering, and feelings of emptiness. If the reason you suffer is your brain — and it is — then your redemption from suffering is also in your brain. Al you need to do is to create a new habit of deliberately feeling joyful.

Once you understand what's going on in your mind from a scientific point of view, you'll find that it's easier to pinpoint what exactly makes you suffer. It's like dealing with pain in your stomach. You're not going to heal the pain with some antacids if what actually hurts is the bullet you were shot with that's embedded in your gut, nor will you prescribe surgery when all you need is a couple of pills to be good as new. In the same vein, we must explore what exactly is going on in your brain, so that we can find an effective, appropriate solution.

The BPD Brain

Neurobiology of behavior is the study of your brain's structure, as well as its chemistry and genetics, and how all of that affects your behavior. This field of science is concerned with the interaction between your brain cells. It studies the way your brain cells create circuitries and neural pathways, with a view to understanding the way information is processed by these pathways, and how all of this affects your behavior. It is impossible to assign all the different sorts of behaviors in BPD to one particular neurobiological cause. Before we really get into this, let's talk about the structures in the brain that you need to be familiar with, as well as basic facts about the brain.

The brain in a full-grown human weighs roughly three pounds and is connected to the spinal cord via the brain stem. The brain stem has nerve cells, also called neurons, which are in bundles.

The cerebrum is the largest part of the brain, with an outer layer known as the cerebral cortex. The cerebral cortex has nerve cells numbering about a hundred billion and is just some millimeters thick.

There are two hemispheres in the cerebrum — left and right. Each hemisphere is divided into four separate lobes: frontal, temporal, parietal, and occipital lobes. Each lobe is assigned very specific behaviors. For planning, decision-making, and coordinating your movements, you need the frontal lobe. The anterior cingulate cortex is behind the frontal lobe, and it handles your heart rate, breathing rate, and blood pressure; it's also pretty active when you're doing exercises in mindfulness like slow breathing.

The hippocampus and amygdala are both rights beneath each of your temporal lobes, deep within your brain. You have your hippocampus to thank or the different kinds of memory you have. As for the amygdala, we'll get into that in detail much later. The temporal lobe houses the region of your brain that handles sound, speech, and hearing.

Behind each hemisphere of your brain is the occipital lobe. This is where you'll find your visual cortex, which is responsible for helping you properly interpret the signals you get from your eyes.

Our focus is going to be on the two parts of the brain, which are intricately involved in BPD: the prefrontal cortex (PFC), which is the region of the brain that sits behind your forehead, and of course, the amygdala, which we will look into right now.

Your Amygdala

Shaped like an almond, this bundle of neurons is embedded deep in each of your brain's hemispheres. The amygdala is the reason you are able to process emotions. So whenever you're in a situation that causes you to react emotionally, it's your amygdala that allows you to figure out what you're feeling, and then to act based on that.

Your amygdala is infamous for handling the fight-or-flight response. As someone with BPD, your amygdala works overtime. This is why you feel things so deeply, and respond as though everything was life and death. It's why you get so upset at the little things, even when they shouldn't warrant such an outburst. Usually, when you take a step back, you can see for yourself that you overreacted, but at the moment, you feel like your reaction is completely justified. The reason for all this is your overactive amygdala.

When it comes to making memories, your amygdala is also involved — especially when said memories have strong emotions attached to them. This is a very useful role that your amygdala plays in regular situations. Say you went to the zoo, and you played with a snake you were told harmless, but then it bit you or wound itself around you tight enough to cause you pain. You feel frightened, and that memory is written in your brain so that you'll never be so willing to put yourself in such a situation again. In terms of evolution, this is good, because this is how you are kept safe and how the human race is able to thrive. As a BPD sufferer, you will find that this evolutionary defense mechanism is in overdrive. So you don't just get a simple warning. What happens is you get that memory replayed in your mind endlessly, even when the threatening situation is over. So you can see it's important that we find ways to regulate the amygdala's actions so that you're not constantly overwhelmed with "all the feels."

It's not every time that you're overcome with unchecked emotions, though. In fact, chances are you experience a lot of moments and situations in which you are just fine, emotionally speaking. It's all down to the context at the end of the day. Not everyone will get to see you at your worst. You might find that it's easier for you to get a grip on yourself when you're at work, but the second you step into your home, all bets are off. As you can probably understand, this causes a lot of confusion for the people around you, as they figure if you can get a hold of your emotions at work, then you can do it anywhere. They don't understand that it really is all down to context, and that home and work are two entirely different situations from a neurobiological standpoint.

Your Prefrontal Cortex

In each brain hemisphere, behind your forehead, lies your prefrontal cortex. That's the part of your brain that calls the shots. It's the executive in charge, so to speak. Some of its roles include:

• **Deciding between right and wrong, or good and evil.** It helps you weigh the pros and cons of your choices, as well as the consequences to yourself and others. *Should I call in sick and skip jury duty? That means I'd be shirking my civic responsibility. On the other hand, I've really got to see what happens next on Game of Thrones.*

• **Helping you mediate conflicting ideas and thoughts.** *On the one hand, you could afford to buy another pair of shoes, but then again, you've already bought ten pairs.*

• **Dealing with social behavior and self-control.** *I really want to scratch my bum, but I'd better not. Not while I'm on this date. Also, no, I definitely should not have sex with that random stranger smiling at me in a children's park.*

• **Making predictions about the future.** *If I don't pay my kid's school fees by tomorrow, then she's going to get kicked out of school, so I'd better forget about buying that piano and focus on paying the fees.*

Now you have all the info on your brain that you need in order to understand BPD. So let's take a look at how these two structures — the amygdala and the prefrontal cortex — work together.

The PFC and the Amygdala — Team Work

Usually, the PFC keeps tabs on the amygdala, in addition to the rest of your limbic system. Here's how that looks like. Let's assume you're wearing a pair of white sneakers that cost you a fortune at your high school reunion. One of your friends who are a little too excited and hyperactive sees you and gives you a hug. In the process, he spills some cranberry juice all over your shoes. Your amygdala notices what just happens, and signals you to go Hulk on your friend. Your hippocampus chimes in as well, reminding you of all the times this particular friend has been so clumsy it cost you one thing or the other, so you get even more upset. You're about to bash his head in with a crowbar that inexplicably appears in your hands when your PFC plays the peacemaker. Your PFC helps you realize the last thing you need is to act out on your anger, because you'll hurt him, and there will be consequences that just wouldn't be worth it.

All of this happens lightning quick in your brain, and without you being consciously aware of it all. Now you know the role each part plays, you can see how it would be terrible if your PFC were damaged in any way, or unable to operate as it should. You would have a lot of trouble controlling your angry impulses. This is the reality of those who have BPD.

The Story Brain Scans Tell

Assault, vandalism, drug abuse, violence, and self-injury all fall under what is termed **impulsive aggression.** There happens to be ample research on impulsive aggression when it comes to BPD. One study, in particular, showed that 47 percent of pyromaniacs and vandals were diagnosed with both Borderline Personality Disorder and Antisocial Personality Disorder. Yet another study showed that the men who were guilty of domestic violence were more likely than not also dealing with BPD, compared to men who never engage in such violence.

Aggression and Your Brain

It's been found that people who are impulsively aggressive more often than not have a PFC that is a tad passive. The same goes for people with BPD, as well. This, of course, is in comparison to people who do not have BPD. The likelihood that the BPD sufferer has a dormant PFC goes up a notch when they also have to deal with PTSD.

BPD and Genes

You may find yourself wondering whether or not BPD is a matter of genes, or simply something that happens on account of the environment. To answer this question, there was a study done on Norwegians, which involved 129 non-identical pairs of twins, as well as 92 identical pairs. The scientists learned that genes could be blamed for about 69 percent of all the BPD symptoms and that the remaining 31 percent could be blamed on factors in the environment. This study closely mirrors the consensus held by most researchers that genes are 60 percent responsible for BPD symptoms, while the environment is responsible for 40 percent.

Now, I know what you're thinking: There's a 60 percent chance you're doomed. However, that is not the case. Do not assume, based on the stats; you're damned to deal with BPD for the rest of your life. The truth is with mindfulness; you'll be able to respond better to circumstances and people in your life, genes be damned. It most definitely will at least help you out with the symptoms that account for the 40 percent.

Brain Chemistry

There are three major chemicals in your brain, which have been extensively studied in the context of BPD: Opiates, serotonin, and cortisol. Let's look at each one.

Opiates: Natural Pain Killers

Whenever there is any damage to your body, internally or externally, your brain comes to your rescue by releasing **opiates** to help numb the pain. They are not so different from the prescription opiate painkillers you get.

It's been found that people who deal with BPD and indulge in self-harm have unnaturally low levels of these opiates, in comparison with the BPD sufferers who do not harm themselves. Ask anyone who's ever had an opiate painkiller, and they will tell you without a moment's hesitation that the drug feels amazing. It boosts feelings of wellbeing. That said, it would make sense to assume that BPD patients who self-injure are actually doing so because they want to bump up the number of opiates coursing through their systems, so they can feel better, albeit for a moment.

According to the research, if you suffer from BPD and you self-harm, then the amount of pain you feel will be nowhere near what a regular person without BPD would feel. So if someone without BPD were to attempt cutting themselves, the pain they would feel would be beyond bearable. Ironically though, BPD sufferers tend to deal with a lot of pain like muscle aches, headaches, back pain, and abdominal pain. They deal with these pains a lot more than people who don't have BPD. It is indeed quite the contradiction.

So how do we explain this? How is it that when people who have BPD cut themselves, they feel very little pain, but at the same time, they have a lot of pain syndromes? One thing to consider is that when the BPD patient cuts, it is usually during or in response to periods of complete emotional stress. In those periods of emotional Dysregulation, the ability to perceive pain drops way below normal. This means when you're not feeling stressed out emotionally, you can feel pain just like everyone else does. Yet another reason that BPD sufferers have to contend with more pain syndromes than usual is that they usually have much poorer health than the average individual.

Serotonin

When it comes to your learning, sleep, and mood regulation, serotonin is key. You can find serotonin not just in the brain, but in the digestive system as well. Serotonin levels have closely tied to such issues as anxiety, poor appetite, and depression. It's not uncommon for sufferers of anxiety and depression to experience symptoms in their stomachs. Most anxiety-prone people have to contend with a condition known as Irritable Bowel Syndrome (IBS) on account of serotonin.

Studies caused scientists to arrive at the conclusion that a lot of people dealing with BPD have abnormally low serotonin levels, and this compounds the issue of impulsive aggression. Low levels of serotonin are also highly correlated with suicidal thoughts and actual attempts.

There are several kinds of medication that all serve the function of upping your brain's serotonin levels. They are especially beneficial to people with anxiety and depression. However, I would be remiss not to mention the fact that they can have undesirable side effects. In fact, if you have too much serotonin in you, this can make you feel even more suicidal than ever before.

Cortisol: The Stress Hormone

Whenever you're stressed out, the hormone cortisol is released. It helps you completely break down carbs and proteins so you can have more oxygen and glucose in your heart, brain, and muscles. Troubles arise when you remain stressed out for a very long period of time. The cortisol builds up in your body and causes your blood pressure to rise. The sugar levels in your body rise as well, and next thing you know, your body is forced to store a lot of unhealthy fat in your stomach. As if all that weren't bad enough, your bones grow thinner and more brittle, and your body is unable to form collagen — the molecule responsible for creating connective tissue and healing your skin.

On top of all that, excess cortisol in your body causes you to age a lot faster than usual. Over time, the cells in your hippocampus begin to go down in number, which means your memory begins to suck, hard.

Now, here's the kicker: People with BPD happen to have the highest cortisol levels, compared to people without BPD. On account of these high cortisol levels, the chances of suicide are multiplied.

We've covered enough about your brain on BPD. Now let's move over to the sunny side.

Your Mindful Brain

The reason mindfulness has helped countless BPD sufferers, past and present, is because it can actually affect the parts of your brain, which we just went over. It can alter your brain's chemistry for the better. Let's see how.

A Better PFC

In the process of being mindful, you will find that your prefrontal cortex is a lot more active than it used to be. It's amazing how much the simple act of paying attention can improve your PFC.

There are various forms of mindfulness, which affect your PFC in many ways. It's not unlike the different kinds of exercises you can do, which benefit your body in a variety of ways. Consistently doing mindfulness exercises keep your brain sharp, focused, and very aware of the present moment. You will find that the brain circuitry responsible for paying attention will be better for it, and your amygdala will benefit too, as it becomes less reactive.

Yoga and Meditation

As a practice, mindfulness meditation is usually taught as simply focusing on your breath. The more you practice, the more your awareness expands. You become aware of more than just your breath, but your very presence, or self.

At the core of a lot of variants of mindfulness, there is an emphasis on the breath. The same is the case in the mindfulness, which you will encounter in DBT. This focus does wonders for you, as it increases the activity in your PFC, and helps you become better at controlling your impulses.

A popular form of mindfulness meditation is known as **Transcendental Meditation (™)**. ; You do this twice a day for twenty minutes each time. The process involves getting your own mantra by way of the Transcendental Meditation Program. As you meditate, your eyes stay shut, and your attention is solely on the mantra you have received.

Those who practice meditation and yoga regularly often report that they feel calm, in body and mind. Studies involving electroencephalography shows the slowing of brain activity in meditators when they sit to meditate. With TM, the slowing is very easy to observe in the mid-portion of the brain, as well as the frontal lobes. The same has also been observed in yoga practitioners. As your brain slows down during TM or certain kinds of yoga, you experience less anxiety. You feel calm and at ease.

If you're not okay with TM or yoga, do not fret. It's been shown that meditative prayer, which is used by various religions all over the world, can have the same effect as transcendental meditation or yoga. I'm not just saying that. There have been studies done on Christians in the process of contemplative prayer. In one study, simply reciting the popular Psalm 23 was more than enough to increase PFC activity. In yet another study, three nuns had their brains scanned. For years, these nuns had practiced **centering prayer** faithfully. Centering prayer is basically focusing on prayer, or a certain Bible verse, with the point being to experience oneness with God. The brain scans of the nuns before and after the prayer showed a remarkable difference. During the prayer, there was an increase in blood flow to the prefrontal cortex — significantly more than when they were not praying.

In Zen Buddhism, you have a practice known as **Zazen**. This is also called the "sitting meditation." There are actual Zazen retreats where, for days, you don't say a word, and you remain sitting for as long as sixteen hours each day. You could try this, but please don't try to take on too much too fast. All you need is 10 to 20 minutes each day for you to reap the benefits. To do Zazen, all you need is to sit down, cross-legged on a comfortable cushion. Place your hands upon your laps, and leave them there. Your eyes must remain open for this one. Your gaze will be focused several feet ahead of you, downwards. The usual thing to focus on would be a Buddhist lesson, but since chances are you aren't a Buddhist, you can simply keep your attention on your inhales and exhales. Do this consistently, and you will reap amazing results.

How Mindfulness Affects Your BPD Brain

As I mentioned earlier, mindfulness has become an indispensable component of modern-day psychotherapy, especially when it comes to Dialectical Behavioral Therapy (DBT), Mindfulness-Based Cognitive Therapy (MBCT), and Mindfulness-Based Stress Reduction (MBSR). That said, there sadly is not enough research on using mindfulness by itself as a way to treat BPD. There has only been one study so far, by Sauer and Baer, published in 2011.

In this study, there were 40 people with BPD. They were all told to write about times when they had gotten exceptionally angry. They only had to write for ten minutes and then stop. When they were done, the researchers took a look at the effects of focused and mindful attention for the short-term, to see how they handled the stress of thoughts about why people treated them poorly. Next, each of the participants was randomly assigned to either continue to think about such thoughts about why people treated them that way, or to simply be mindful and self-focused for some time. Next, they were given a task to see how well they would handle distress. The group who were mindful were able to handle the distress a lot better than those who were focused on their anger, and also stated that they felt a lot less angry after the meditation period.

If anything, this single experiment shows that you can indeed experience significant benefits from deliberately practicing mindfulness. Don't be dismayed about the fact that there is just one study. The fact is that there are myriads of studies that have been conducted on the use of mindfulness in conjunction with other treatment modalities to help people who have BPD, and in each of these studies, the proof is irrefutable that mindfulness multiplies the beneficial effects greatly.

Chapter Five: Practicing Mindfulness

There's no way that you could learn a new skill without any form of guidance or instruction. Imagine you're given the keys to a Ferrari, and you're asked to drive it in really heavy traffic, but you've never driven a day in your life. That would not work out well. The same thing applies when it comes to mindfulness. If it were simply a matter of telling you, "Go forth and be mindful," then I had better wrap up this book here because there's nothing else to do, I guess. Don't worry. I'm not going to leave you hanging.

At the core of Dialectical Behavioral Therapy is mindfulness. What we're going to do is take a look at each of the steps you need to go through to practice mindfulness. It's not enough to know it can help you. I want to empower you with the knowledge you need to save yourself.

Now, you may be a tad skeptical of all of this. Perhaps more than a few times already, you have considered setting this book aside, because you find it inconceivable that simply learning mindfulness as a skill could be all you need to turn your life around. It's not unusual for BPD patients to be skeptical of the whole thing. For a problem as complex as BPD, how could anyone possibly even suggest something as simple and basic as mindfulness? What the heck does "mindfulness" even mean anyway? Full of mind? You're tempted to assume it's some religious hokey by Buddhists, and so you should not pay it any attention. There is no way all your problems could be resolved by simply breathing, you think. These are all logical thoughts.

It's natural to raise a brow in suspicion at the whole concept, especially when you have no idea what it really means to practice mindfulness, or how you would even begin in the first place.

Once you know what to do, it becomes easier for you to accept the idea. However, knowledge is not enough. Knowledge is not power. It's the application of the knowledge that will give you all the healing you seek. Just because you know the mechanics do not mean you really know how to work it. The only way to truly know is to practice what you do know. By practice, I do not mean you should try it once or twice. I mean, you should dedicate yourself to being consistent about your mindfulness practice. This is the only way you can truly reap the benefits and get better. It's not unlike working out. You don't expect one day at the gym to undo years of terrible dieting and a lazy lifestyle. You have to keep going regularly. You need to keep training the same muscles over and over again until they get better and stronger. To keep said muscles, you'll need to make working out a lifestyle. The same applies to mindfulness.

Most people who have BPD tend to resort to stopgap measures like cutting, reckless behavior, and other things like that. The problem is these measures are beyond ineffective in the long run. The relief you get in the moment is short-lived, and sooner or later, you will do yourself or some other person irreparable harm. What's the alternative then? Mindfulness. In the practice of mindfulness, you will find long-lasting peace and calm. You will find a more effective solution that can serve you at all times. It will take a bit of time and practice, and you will need to be patient, but in the end, it will pay off.

Laying The Groundwork

You're probably trying to figure out how often and for how long each time you should practice being mindful. Since you're only just starting out, it's best for you to begin with just 15 to 20 minutes a day. You can easily split that up into two sessions, once at the start of your day, and once at the end.

As you get used to your practice, you could begin to add on a bit of time to your sessions each day. We're going to cover ways in which you can be mindful all through your day, but we're also going to cover the basics on picking a set time each day for a more focused, formal session. This is important because being deliberate about it is the only way you can get better at being mindful. One more thing I ought to mention is that no matter how good you become at being mindful, you must make sure you keep up your practice day after day.

As for when you should practice, you could do this once in the morning and once in the night, as I previously mentioned. However, this is not a prerequisite. Find a time that is convenient for you and commit to it. If you find that you're exhausted at the end of your day, then you definitely would be better off practicing in the afternoon or in the morning. If you have to start your mornings early and have a lot to do to prepare your family for the day, then you might want to consider noon or night for practice. It's all up to you. The point is you must make it a habit, and remember, the only way habits are formed by constant repetition. Do what you need to in order to make it happen. Leave yourself a note somewhere you'll always pass by, so you can remember, or set a reminder on your phone.

For a lot of people, it helps to practice mindfulness in a certain spot every time. Like I already mentioned, you don't absolutely have to, but it does help to have a sacred space for it. Eventually, though, you will be able to practice mindfulness wherever you find yourself.

Another question that plagues those who are new to mindfulness is what pose or posture they should adopt. Should they sit or stand or something? There are a number of different mindfulness practices. For some of them, you will need to be seated, and for others, you will have to move about a bit. You do not necessarily have to adopt the lotus position if you find that a little tough on your knees.

If it's a seated mindfulness practice, then it would be best to adopt a posture where your chest is open, meaning you keep your arms away from your chest. You also want to make sure that your bottom is firmly and evenly planted on the seat. Choose a good chai, which allows you to sit up comfortably. If you need a few pillows to support your back, then use them. Make sure your feet are flat on the floor, firmly and evenly. Do not cross your ankles or your legs. Your shoulders must be back and upright. Don't hunch over. You may keep your arms on your lap. If you like, you can turn your palms upwards. A huge part of this mindfulness practice is also aware of your posture as you sit. Now that you know how to sit, you're going to practice while keeping your eyes open.

Owning Your Mind

The more you practice mindfulness, the more you'll find that you own your mind. You are more in control of it. Right now, I can see how you'd think this is an impossible feat. However, it's true! As you practice, you will discover you are not your emotions or your thoughts, but something more.

In the DBT space, there's something known as the **emotion mind**. What this means is that your emotions dictate the thoughts that you think. As someone with BPD, you feel like you're constantly being tossed about by intense feelings that are seemingly beyond your control. You go along with them, with very detrimental consequences. Each time you look back on your actions, you can't quite figure out how you got to the point where you reacted the way you did. You find your inability to pay attention makes you more likely to change your mind on account of your feelings, and so you do not keep the commitments you've made to yourself and others. So you find yourself killing relationships, which you value, and saying things you do not mean.

For the most part, people tend to ignore how much of a habit thought patterns are. We never really think about our thinking, because we weren't taught how to do that. This is where mindfulness can help again. If your mind is not trained, it can cause you a lot of pain and heartache without you even being aware of it. Like a pendulum, you swing from one extreme to the other. You either get so enmeshed in your mind that you pay way too much attention to certain thoughts, or you worry to the point of obsession and are unable to see past your nose. Either way, you don't pay attention to your thinking habits. It almost seems to you that things tend to unfold on their own, and you have no power over the way you react. I don't need to tell you how being on one extreme or the other can cause you issues, and suffering. Mindfulness will help you grow in curiosity, awareness, and attention. This is how you'll finally own your mind and break the habits of thought you've got.

The Need for Curiosity and Attentiveness

When you don't develop your attention, and when you're not curious about life, you'll be stuck in your usual routines. Routines may help you avoid the pain you feel, but in the end, they also keep you stuck, and this can add to more pain in the long run. It never pays to try to ignore your emotions and thoughts.

You have to pay attention to your thoughts. This means you need to pause every now and then and take an unbiased look at your mind. How fast or slow are you thinking? Are your thoughts a jumbled mess or well put together? Are they loving and kind or angry and resentful? What exactly is it that you're thinking about?

The point of mindfulness is to take charge of your mind and thought processes, and by extension, your emotions. AS you pay attention, the peace and serenity you feel in your life will go up a hundredfold. It might be difficult to believe that mindfulness can help you achieve all this, especially as you've never done it before, but I promise you it works.

The Practice

As you practice, pay attention to how your body and mind feel. This will help you learn all the things you can do to decrease your suffering through your emotions and thoughts. In the DBT space, these actions are known as the "what" and "how" skills — "what" being the actions you take to be mindful, and "how" being the way you go about it.

Try the practices that you will be given in this book at least one time. You'll need a journal, so you can take down notes on your experiences after each practice. You will find that some of the practices feel better for you than others, however, don't stick to them just yet without trying out everything, so that you can tell what works for you and what doesn't. The goal isn't to get you to like the practice, but to encourage you to become more curious, and give your mind a challenge.

I need to point out that some days, you will feel your practice went a lot better than on other days. This does not mean you're failing. It's just the way it is. Today you're breezing through your practice; tomorrow, you're finding the same practice challenging. The beauty of mindfulness is that your experience of it is always dynamic, never static.

One more thing I should mention is that your mind will wander. You must be comfortable with that fact. When you notice your mind has gone off on a tangent, do not beat up on yourself. Noticing is actually progress! So simply bring your mind back to your mindful task, whatever it may be. Each time your mind wanders, and you bring it back, you will get better at maintaining mindfulness. Remember, your mind is like a muscle. This is how it gets stronger.

The Power of Intention

You cannot practice mindfulness without intention. The intention is a beautiful thing, because if you can do something mindlessly, then with intention, you can actually do it mindfully. Intention means you're choosing to pay attention to something, with a specific goal in mind. So you could brush your teeth like always, while your thoughts are on autopilot, wondering about bills and mortgages, or you can spend that time noticing the way you brush, the way your mouth feels, and so on. You notice the desire to think about how to take care of the bills, but then you shift your attention back to the simple act of brushing your teeth. As you brush, your mind will wander off. When it does, you can simply come back to brushing. You can do this with any activity that you do on the regular, whether it's driving, walking, doing the dishes, or laundry. This is how you infuse mindfulness in your daily activities.

There is a misconception that the whole point of mindfulness is to have a mind that never wanders. That's impossible. You will always have thoughts in your head. That's the function of your brain. What mindfulness is, is intentionally choosing to refocus your attention back on the tasks at hand each time your mind wanders. It's not about keeping your mind quiet and empty.

Decide, Commit, Succeed

As you make the decision to practice being mindful, you've got to keep reminding yourself of what you've set out to do and why. It matters that in the beginning, you are clear with yourself about the fact that you're going to be mindful of what the task you've chosen, whether it's doing the dishes or washing your car. Tell yourself you will do this mindfully, and automatically your brain takes a cue that it needs to focus on the task before you. Once you commit this way, you are more likely to succeed.

A Different Practice for Each Day

All you need to do is intend to change at least one of the things you do habitually for every day, just for a week. If you're used to getting out of bed on the left side, try getting out on the right. Do you usually open doors with your dominant hand? Commit to using the other hand. It's all about doing something different for a set period of time and paying full attention to the process.

Observing

Yet another skill the practice of mindfulness will give you is observation. You will begin to simply observe and notice the thoughts you have and the way you feel. In DBT, this is known as the "observe" skill.

In the practice of mindfulness, you're not observing with the goal of passing judgment or labeling things. You're simply paying attention to your experience, without trying to assign it to a box. You experience whatever is happening fully, with all your senses. The challenge here is not labeling anything.

For the most part, we do everything we do without paying much attention to it, and this is why we miss out on very critical bits of information that could make our experience better. As you learn to pay attention, the automatic response you're so used to will become apparent to you. This is particularly useful for those with BPD since a huge part of the problem with BPD is the thoughtless, automatic reactions that cause needless suffering. If you find that there is something or someone to whom you naturally respond with anger, as you become more mindful, you'll notice that it's simply an automatic response you've gotten used to on account of repetition, which has made it a habit. Then you will find that you actually have a choice. You can choose to respond differently, the same way you chose to start lacing your right shoe first before your left in your mindfulness practices.

One more superpower that mindfulness will give you is the ability to notice your emotions in the beginning stages before they fully blossom. Once you're able to tell you're getting sad or angry before you fully give in to the emotion, you will no longer feel as though emotions "just happen" to you. You will realize you're in control. You'll realize that at any point in time, you can redirect your emotions. No longer will you be ambushed by intense emotions.

Simply observing is an amazing way to calm your mind. Now, this can be quite a challenge, especially as you will not need words. We tend to assign words to everything we experience. For practice, simply try being outside by yourself, noticing the sights and sounds, without actually assigning any words to them. In the beginning, this will not be easy. Can you just imagine seeing a red rose, without the need to call it "a red rose" in your mind? It's not easy at first, but over time, you get better at it. As you simply observe with no labeling or judging, the part of your mind responsible for thinking will quiet down, and shut off. This is the part of your mind that gets hyperactive whenever you feel anxious or stressed out. The simple act of watching, observing, and noticing, will calm both your body and mind immensely. It involves moving from a state of action, doing, and thinking, to a simple state of **being**, unconditioned by anything internal or external.

As you get better at the art of observation, you will find that you can watch and notice the thoughts flying about in your head without getting all tangled up in them. In doing this, your mind slows down, and you feel calmer than ever. You no longer feel the need to analyze or understand every single thing, or to solve problems you perceive which may not actually be there. You're good with just watching the thoughts fly in and out, as though you were a tree, and the thoughts are birds, just flying about, not affecting you in any way.

As I mentioned earlier, your brain is responsible for creating thoughts. That's its role, and there's nothing wrong with that at all. If you wouldn't judge your heart for moving blood around your body, or your lungs for moving oxygen into your body and carbon dioxide out, then you shouldn't judge your brain for doing what it does either. You don't get mad at the blood, or the air so doesn't be mad at your thoughts. Just always remember that you are not your thoughts. They come, and they go. You are the observer. You get to decide whether or not you want to act on those thoughts at all times. The process of mindfulness will help you come to that realization fully.

Busy Mind

There are times when it can be a complete inconvenience to have an overactive mind. It's always busy with distractions and unpleasant stuff. Let's take a look at the process of rumination, where your mind is focused on one situation only, and won't give it a rest. It can be incredibly difficult to get a grip on. Countless hours are wasted as you rehash some experience over and over. You become obsessed with whatever it was that happened and even depressed. You get fearful as well, over bogeymen that don't exist. This is even tougher if you're a perfectionist with BPD. Perfectionism and BPD are a cocktail potent enough to keep you from ever taking action, no matter how important it is that you do something.

Yet another phenomenon that plagues the busy mind is the process of catastrophizing, which is exactly what it sounds like. You make things out to be more dangerous or worse than it really is, and all you can imagine are the various ways in which things could go wrong, and then some. Let's say you went for a job interview, and you were not accepted for some reason or the other. Rather than keep applying to other organizations, you come to the conclusion that no one is ever going to take you on as an employee. You take that a step further to mean you're going to lose your home, your car, and everything you own, basically. You go a step further and decide it means you're going to starve to death. It may seem a tad dramatic now as you read this in a calm state of mind, but this is the reality of the mind of a BPD sufferer whose mind is used to catastrophizing things. This kind of thinking sends your anxiety and stress levels through the roof. The good thing is that there is a fix: Mindfulness. It helps you learn to laugh at yourself and not to take things so seriously.

Your Senses

As you observe, engage all senses. You'll find that the things you're watching will change, for good, or bad. Or they'll change to something just neutral. You can simply observe the changes without becoming attached to them. Get an orange, cut it in half, and smell it. Put a bit of salt in your mouth, and really get into the taste. Notice the way it kind of hits you with a bit of a slap, then evens out. You might even notice a barely perceptible sweetness to it as the salty taste wears away. Go outside in a pair of shorts and a sleeveless shirt, and really pay attention to the temperature. Notice the way it feels on your skin. Notice the tiny little fluctuations, moments of cold in the heat, and heat in the cold. Go sit in a nice park, and simply watch people without turning your head. Allow them to come into and out of your point of view. Don't try to follow them with your eyes, either. Simply focus on the space in front of you. Remember, we've already mentioned you will get distracted. When you notice, know that it's okay and simply bring your attention back to the task at hand.

Observe the Urge

A lot of times, as you observe something happening, you get the urge to do something about it. For example, your nose may feel itchy right now. The impulse is to scratch it. It makes sense. You do it without thinking and then move on. But what if you didn't? What if you just noticed the need to scratch the itch, but did nothing about it? This is yet another way to practice mindfulness.

You feel the need to do something about what you're observing, particularly when what you're observing is causing you to feel intense emotions, on account of the thoughts the situation inspires in you. In the DBT space, there is a lot of focus on urges to act. One of the most important roles emotions play is to get you to act. The way that you act is not part and parcel of the emotion, but the urge you feel is completely driven by the feelings you have.

At times you're prompted to act in ways that do not serve you. The behaviors you're being driven to do not align with your goals, or could have negative effects in the end. With that said, it's important that you develop the ability to notice the emotion and the urges you feel, and choose not to act upon them. In order to make this your practice, deliberately notice things, notice the urge you feel to do something, and then choose to do nothing. Are you a neat freak? Did someone leave a can of soda and an open pack of Doritos on the floor? In this situation, I'm certain you'd feel the need to clean up the mess or to ask them to clean it up. Don't. Simply observe the urge and let it pass. I'm not asking you to become a slob. I'm merely asking you to try an exercise, which will help you not to act on urges that have made your life a nightmare so far.

Think back to times when if you had simply resisted the urge to act, things would have turned out different, and better. Think of that one time you yelled at the cashier because you were impatient. How could you have handled that better, knowing what you know now? Sure, you could have felt the emotion of anger because they were so slow, and you could have felt the urge to yell your head off at them. However, now you know you do not need to act on your urges. It's not enough to know. You must practice as well. So let those itches go without scratching. Notice your natural impulses, and just let them go.

Suppression and Enhancement

We typically react to our thoughts and feelings by either suppressing them or enhancing them. When you get an urge or a certain thought, you could suppress it by putting the kibosh on it, thinking to yourself, "I really shouldn't be thinking this way, or thinking about this at all for that matter. What a terrible thought!" This is not the best way to deal with your thoughts and emotions. What happens when you attempt to suppress them is that you make them all the more intense. You lose your power, giving it away to the thought or emotion plaguing you. If I asked you not to think about a blue elephant, what do you think is going to happen? You just saw a blue elephant in your mind's eye, didn't you? This is why suppression simply doesn't work.

On the other hand, you could choose to respond by enhancing the thought or emotion. By enhancing it, you make it bigger than it really is. So when you've got a particularly painful thought, you take it and dial it up to 100. You create needless suffering for yourself. Next thing you know, you're taking action

84

on urges that you feel, and nine times out of ten, the actions you do choose are detrimental to you and everyone else involved.

The Dangers of Collecting Evidence

If you do not practice simply observing your thoughts and emotions without taking action on the urges, then you're going to find yourself constantly collecting evidence to support the painful thoughts and emotions you're entertaining. Your evidence will be anything but concrete, more often than not. It will simply be a collection of memories, experiences, thoughts, and emotions, altered to for the narrative you're entertaining in your mind — whatever it takes to make you think you're right to feel the way you do at the moment. What this inevitably leads to is pain and suffering.

The way to avoid doing this is by being mindful. You've simply got to pay attention. This is how you gain control of your mind, and stop letting it boss you around. This is one more reason to continue with the exercise of simply observing and noticing. In the process, you will glean some insight as to how your mind operates. You will come to know who you really are, and the totality of your thoughts and emotions.

I want to make it clear that practicing mindfulness does not mean you will be happy forever and always. There will be moments when you're feeling down. Mindfulness will help you notice when you're feeling down, but it will help you deal with it in a healthier way because you'll understand innately that it's not permanent, and that it's okay. You'll also notice all the amazing things you've experienced, but never really realized were worth reveling in. You'll notice all the beauty and wonder you had always missed because you were stuck in your murky thoughts.

Emotions Don't Last

Neurology has shown something very interesting about emotions: If you leave them alone, neither enhancing them nor suppressing them, they really don't last all that long. The lifespan of an emotion that is not tampered with is anything from five seconds to twenty seconds flat. So when you feel an emotion, if you just leave it alone without making it worse by catastrophizing, or attempting to suppress it, it goes away. Thinking about the painful experience over and over simply gives the emotion more time to grow and take over your mind.

Do you seek to ease your suffering? Then learn to let things go. Do not become so attached to your emotions and thoughts. This is something the Buddhists have known for thousands of years. Do not hold on. Allow them to float away, and you'll find your suffering taking flight right along with them.

Releasing by Watching

All you need to do is watch. Observe, and you'll find that the feelings and thoughts that seem to plague you only do so because you hold them in place. You'll notice that they come around, spend very little time, and are off again. They're like the weather, but even more unstable. Just like the clouds in the sky, the emotions and thoughts you had in the past can roll around again. However, you can have the wind blow them away by the simple act of letting go.

The reason you have thoughts that insist on making a home in your head and bringing strangers in with them is that you've got a strong emotional connection to them. It's why the thought of a lime won't stick in your mind, but think about that one time your mother yelled at you and embarrassed you in public, and suddenly, the thought just doesn't want to go without a fight, it seems. This is why it's incredibly difficult to give up memories, be they good or bad.

As difficult as it is, if you intend to stop suffering, then you will need to learn how to let go. It's difficult. I won't even kid you about that. Yet it can be done, and it **should** be done. This doesn't mean you can never revisit a thought or a memory; it's just important that you know you can choose not to at any point in time, and that you can choose when and how you think about it all.

If you want to get better at dealing with the emotions that cause you pain, then it doesn't get better than the practice of observing and noticing, where you intentionally allow yourself to experience the emotions which hurt you or terrify you, so you can get better at handling them. It's a gradual process where you are exposed to triggers, from the least intense to the most intense, until you're eventually able to observe the feelings you have, with no suffering attached.

In mindfulness, to "watch and attend" means to focus on exactly what is in the moment, and nothing more. You're focused on everything going on right now without adding to it or taking from it. All your thoughts, sensations, and emotions will ebb and flow. It's all in a constant state of flux. Knowing that what you do in this exercise is simply watch, notice all that is in the presence, and then you will notice the changes, which happen.

It may seem like it's pretty much the same thing as reliving the experience, but this is a far cry from that. It is like the difference between acting in a movie and watching the movie. One is immersive; the other is not. You get to realize as you watch and attend, that you are not your emotions, thoughts, desires, or sensations. You notice that all of these things come and go, and only one thing remains: The observer: You.

Chapter Six: Mindfulness Practices

Without further ado, let's get right to the various mindfulness practices, so you can begin the work of reclaiming your life.

Taste

Take a piece of fruit, candy, chocolate, or some jelly or something and put it in your mouth. Keep it there for two minutes, minimum. As it's in your mouth, pay attention to it. What does it taste like, really? Don't try to label the taste; just experience it. What's the texture like? Does the taste change over time? Does it become more intense, less intense, or somewhat different? Notice your experience. Observe the thoughts and emotions, which pass through your mind as you hold this food in your mouth. When you find your mind has wandered — and it will — simply bring your attention back to the food in your mouth, and continue to notice.

Smell

Get some essential oil, or a piece of fruit, or a flower, or a fragrant cream. It doesn't matter what you get as long as it has a scent. Now, for two minutes, pay attention to the way that it smells. Bring it close to your nose. How does it smell? Now take it far from your nose. How does it smell now? Slowly move the object closer, then further, and observe the way the smell changes or doesn't change all that much. What do you feel, as you smell this? Notice your reaction. Pay attention to the thoughts that flit about your mind as you smell the object in your hand. If your mind wanders, be glad you noticed, and return to the task at hand.

Touch

There are several ways to practice mindfulness through touch, and we're going to cover a couple of them. Put your hands together. Make sure you've got your palms and fingers of each hand well lined up so that they're pressing against each other. Next, slide your hands against each other back and forth for just 20 seconds. As you do this, notice the way it feels, in terms of texture. Notice the temperature, the way it changes from regular to heated.

After 20 seconds, stop rubbing your palms together. Take the next 30 seconds to observe simply. Notice the way your hands feel. Notice the sensations and the temperature. Notice the way you feel emotionally.

Another mindfulness practice with touch is simply to notice when you have an itch. For two minutes, do nothing about the itch. Don't scratch. Just watch and attend. Notice the sensations caused by the itch. Notice the urges you feel to reach out and take care of it. Notice the emotions that come up. Do nothing until the two minutes are up. Ideally, you should do each of these touch practices for up to three minutes at a time.

Sound

Go out to a park, or sit in your yard at the front or the back. You'll be sitting for 20 minutes. While you're there, focus on the sounds around you. Focus your attention on nature's sounds. Do not try to label them, simply notice them as sounds, and nothing more. Forget about figuring out what they mean, or trying to identify them. Just notice, are the sounds low, or high pitched? Are they soft sounds or loud? Are continuous or intermittent? Pay attention. Your mind will definitely wander. Be thankful when you notice you've gone off, and then bring your attention gently back. Never beat up on yourself no matter how often you zone out and forget to be mindful.

Sight

To practice mindfulness using your sight, take a couple of minutes, or three, to observe your hand. Look at it as though it were new to you. Look at it like something you're not remotely familiar with since you've never seen such a thing before. The whole point behind this is to watch and attend to all the details and features of your hand that you can see. Look at the back of your hand, as well as your palm. Observe your fingers, and all the lines and creases on your hand. Observe the skin colors. This exercise will be quite interesting to you because you use your hands for so much, and so often that you never even give them a second thought. As you do this exercise, you might find you don't know the back of your hand, as well as that saying, would have you think you do.

Labeling

Now that we have covered the essential skill of observing and noticing, we're going to move on to yet another important skill: Labeling. This is the act of taking your experience and putting words to it.

What labeling helps us do, is it allows us to classify our experiences. This helps us when we want to share said experiences with others, as well as ourselves. In DBT, this is basically the "describe" skill.

Usually, both noticing and labeling are skills that are used to complement each other. Before you can label your thoughts, emotions, and sensations, you must first notice them. Only then can you label them from a mindful place. For a lot of people, it's a lot easier to learn the labeling skill than the noticing skill.

Labeling matters, as nothing causes us more suffering than the labels we tag our experiences with. If you label your experiences negatively, then you will definitely feel distressed each time it comes to mind. So what we're going to do now is to learn how to label your emotions, sensations, and thoughts in a mindful manner, so that the result is little to no suffering at all.

"The table is crooked," "The cereal is soggy," "The dog is white," are various examples of what labeling is about when using facts. In the same way, you can label your emotions. More often than not, your emotions are either judged harshly, or completely invalidated on account of the labels you choose to give them. The trouble is that the judgments you pronounce on your emotions only serve to make the emotions even more intense and increase your discomfort in the end.

"I feel anger," "My belly feels tense," "My throat feels like there's a huge lump in it" are various nonjudgmental ways you can label what you're feeling in the moment. These labels are based on the facts, which cannot be disputed. As you label, you must only give words to the sensations, emotions, and thoughts that you're having at present. There is no need for extra commentary, and you do not have to play judge and jury over them.

Let's assume you've come downstairs for breakfast, and there's a bowl of cereal waiting for you. You've had a spoonful, and it's soggy. If you were to label the experience simply, all you would say is, "This cereal is soggy." However, if you were to add that "I think it's soggy because my wife deliberately made it way before she called me down to have some because she's upset with me that I didn't take out the trash that one time back in 1998," then that would be you playing judge. You're making assumptions and arriving at a conclusion that others would objectively not even come to, were they to observe what you're observing at the moment. They would agree with you that the cereal is soggy, but as for the imagined conflict between you and your wife, they wouldn't be so quick to agree with you on that. It's not that your assumptions may not be spot on sometimes, but seeing as the fact before we are that your cereal is soggy, that's all we want to label.

Labeling is the best way to handle your emotions. Let's say you constantly suffer from anxiety. The usual thought process is something along the lines of, "Oh crap, I feel anxious. Again. Man I hate this. Why do I always get so anxious? I can't believe the level of anxiety I have right now. This is terrible! I can't do anything about it. When the heck will it be over? I really can't put up with this for much longer. Man, I'm so anxious!" On and on this thought pattern goes, feeding on itself, an ouroboros, unending. The more attention you feed this thought pattern, the more your anxiety goes up. How would labeling help here?

The better thing to do would be first to notice how you're feeling at the moment. As soon as you notice it, label it, sticking as close to the facts as you possibly can. Here's what that would sound like: "I feel anxious. My heart rate has gone up. My breathing rate has increased, as well. My palms are moist with sweat. My thoughts are moving too fast. I also feel hot."

The difference here is that we first noticed the anxiety, and then we labeled it appropriately by using precise words to explain all that was happening at the moment. This way, you allow the anxiety to do its thing and then blow over, without unintentionally enhancing it or making it out to be more than it is. Labeling helps you remain grounded in the facts, keeping you from being swept away by the tide of emotions and thoughts, which threaten to drown you at the moment.

Making Use of Words

For a moment, I want you to imagine an animal you've never come across before. Next, you're going to take this experience —

the encounter — as a chance to practice being mindful. You would word the experience this way: "This animal is brown and black. It comes up to my knees in height. It has a lot of furs and seems to enjoy eating bones. It makes holes in the ground, and when you throw an object away from you, it runs to get it and bring it back to you. It makes a hoarse sound, and has a tail it wags every so often." Now, this animal would be clearly labeled by others like a dog, but if you genuinely were clueless about what a dog looks like, you've still perfectly described it anyway. There is no judgment in your description. It's a simple statement of the facts. This is what you're going for when you practice mindfulness by labeling.

Thoughts Do Not Equal Facts

You now know that labeling is all about noticing what you're experiencing within and without, and then putting words to what you have noticed. This is awareness, at its most basic level. Let's assume you're going on a road trip to a different state to visit family, and you're not a big fan of packing or road trips. But you feel you have got to make the trip, or everyone would be so disappointed that you're a no-show for the second time in a row.

Next thing you know, your stomach begins to act funny. You're a lot hotter than usual. You worry that you won't be able to make the trip, or that you're going to have to abort halfway through.

You pack up your stuff anyway, but then your stomach makes a funny noise, and you think to yourself, "I don't think I can make this trip." That statement right there is anything but a fact. It's simply a thought, and nothing more. The fact is you actually might be able to make the trip, even if you think you couldn't. This is why it matters that you label things according to the facts.

Here's what factual labeling would sound like: "I have to make this trip. I have noticed that I'm feeling anxious about this trip. I can also see that I think if I don't make it, I will be thought of as a disappointment." Notice the way this labeling makes it sound as though you're a third party observing yourself, much like a dispassionate researcher.

Labeling, like noticing, is a great way to learn about your thought process. You will learn about yourself, and this will help you have even more control of your life. When you know that your thoughts are just thoughts and nothing more, you will feel even more empowered and will make better choices for yourself. It's only a thought that you cannot make the trip, or that your family would be disappointed in you for not showing up. It's only a thought, not the truth.

The Facts, And Only the Facts

Labeling relies heavily on you, sticking to the facts. Beyond relying on facts only, there is the element of doing away with judgment. A lot of us are guilty of judging most of the time. When you pass judgment on something or someone, it's basically like taking a shortcut to describe something you experienced properly or to help others understand what you mean exactly. There's nothing wrong with that; however, it's useful to keep in mind that when we make judgments about whether something is right or wrong, it's all based on our personal perspective, even if we never come right out to say what that is.

As an example, your friend might ask you about a party you attended, and you might reply, "It was a bore." Based on your response, your friend could very well decide not to attend such parties, or not to attend parties thrown by that particular host of the party you called "a bore." However, if you were to label t mindfully, you would have responded by saying something like, "It really kicked off by 8 PM. There was a lot of food and even more drinks. The music was loud, and the place was packed." Now, you might hate all of that, because you're not a party person or something, but it's possible that your friend would love all of that at a party. So it was a bore to you, but they could find it exciting. When you label your experiences properly, you do away with biases, and it makes it easier for people to communicate with you.

Chapter Seven: Even More Mindfulness Practices

In this chapter, we're going to cover some more mindfulness practices, which you should be able to engage in wherever, whenever.

Having a Meal

The great thing about this mindfulness practice is that you get to do it every day since you've got to eat something each day. So the next time you sit at your table to eat, do it as mindfully as you can. The goal here is to apply the skill of labeling to your mealtime experience. First, you want to put words to what it's like to sit at the table. You want to talk about the facts and only the facts.

In doing this, you'll describe the table you're sitting at, as well as the chair you're sitting on. You'll describe what the table placement is like, as well as the plate that you've got in front of you.

From there, move on to the food you've got on your plate. Describe it. What does it look like? What does it smell like?

Next, take a bite out of it. What does your food taste like? What's the texture like in your mouth?

Keep in mind that you're doing all the labeling in your mind, not saying it aloud. The last thing we need is for you to choke as you practice. Just do this all in your mind, devoting the entirety of your attention to the experience of eating at the table, right here and now when your mind wanders as it is bound to do, know that it's awesome you noticed! Them, gently return your attention to your meal, noticing it, and labeling it as you eat.

Watching a Flower

This exercise will take two minutes each time, tops. Just look at a flower, as though you've never seen it before. As you observe it, notice its scent. Can you put a label on what you're smelling? What would you call the colors you can see on the flower? What sort of emotions does the flower elicit from you, if any at all? Take your time with this, drinking in all the details with your senses. It's easy to get bored by this or to give in to distractions. That's alright. When you notice you're losing interest or attention, simply come back to the flower, and resume with your labeling practice. You can repeat the labels if need be. The whole point is to simply practice proper labeling while keeping your mind focused on one goal.

Bothersome Thoughts

For this exercise, find a quiet spot where you will not be disturbed and take a seat. Make sure you are as comfortable as you can be. Next, recall something that bothers you, something that you've been worried about for a while. Be careful to choose something that isn't incredibly worrisome, or that won't trigger high levels of anxiety. It needs to be just enough to worry about, but not enough to make you quit the practice altogether.

Next, simply notice all the emotions you feel about this subject. Just watch the anxiety and whatever else that comes up. Label everything that happens to you physically, from your breathing to your heart rate, to the way your chest feels, or the tension in your body. Notice and label the thoughts going through your mind. Do this for four minutes tops, or until you feel your anxiety begin to drop, and you're back to feeling the same way you did before you began the practice (or even better!) This is one practice I recommend you do every day.

Labeling Emotions

This exercise will take you two minutes each time. All you're going to do is sit, and then mindfully notice and label one emotion. First, notice all the judgments that you have when it comes to this emotion. Once you're through with that, get rid of the judgmental labels, and then relabel your emotions nonjudgmentally. As you do, just be aware of the way your body feels, as the emotion courses through you. Describe the feeling as best you can. You can do this with all sorts of emotions. It helps if you've got your journal handy, so you can jot down all that you've observed with each session and emotion. As you go about your day, whenever the emotions you've covered in your mindfulness practice come up, take the opportunity to repeat the practice again. As you label the emotions, pay attention to whether there are any changes, no matter how subtle they may seem.

Labeling Ads

Grab a magazine, and find an ad in it. It's got to be one you find visually appealing. For only two minutes, label what you can see in the ad. Only focus on the facts. Don't get subjective here. When your two minutes are up, flip through the magazine for an ad you do not like, for whatever reason. Spend a couple of minutes here as well, as you label the ad.

Chapter Eight: Non Judgment and Acceptance

In the previous chapter, we talked about the skills of noticing and labeling. Now we're going to get into what it means to label with no judgment, and after that, we will get into acceptance and what it really means.

If you've ever met with a therapist who is an expert in DBT, or if you've ever gone far in studying mindfulness or meditation, then you no doubt will be familiar with non-judgment.

At the very center of the practice of mindfulness is non-judgment. This is also a huge part of DBT mindfulness as well. The ability to become aware of your judgments, and then release them, is a major factor in successfully practicing mindfulness. Now, you may consider yourself to be the least judgmental person you know, but you may need to give that a rethink. For the most part, a large number of us are unaware of the fact that we judge more often than not. The world is a judgmental place. You can see it in every aspect of life, whether it's in business, economics, politics, religion, and even at home.

Passing judgment is a habit that a lot of us have to contend with. If we're going to change this habit, then the first step is to notice when we pass judgments, to begin with. As you pay full attention to the judgments you pass, you will find that they tend to mold your thoughts, emotions, and attitudes. In order to hone this skill, all you need to do is begin noticing something. Do this with no form of evaluation whatsoever. By this, I mean you do not label anything as of right or wrong, good or bad, awesome or terrible, should be or shouldn't be. You simply remain neutral and detached from the opinions you hold, other people's views, and the need for approval or the fear of disapproval. Simply stick with the facts of the matter, just like you would do with labeling. Before we proceed with exercises in non-judgment, let's take a closer look at what judgments are, and how they work. This matters, because otherwise, you'll be judging yourself for judging, which would defeat the purpose of this exercise.

The Issue with Judgments

Let us take a critical look at the issue with judgments. First of all, there are times when judgment has no problem whatsoever. That said, for the most part, when you adopt a judgmental point of view and combine that with negative feelings, you will find it to be a destructive cocktail both to yourself and to others around you. Your relationships will suffer for it. When you pass judgment without even a second thought, it means that your mind is completely made up of an issue or a person. This is not so bad when it's a positive judgment, as it's rare that a positive judgment would cause you grief, to begin with. However, when judgment is negative — especially when it comes to a desire for the current reality to be something other than what it is — then this is where the bulk of your suffering comes from.

The point being made here is that judgments never allow any leeway for you to be curious about people or life in general since your mind is completely made up. AS a sufferer of BPD, judgment shows up even more often for you than for others, in a myriad of ways. This is especially the case if you're struggling with emotions, you just can't stand any longer, or if you like to think in black-and-white. All that judgment does, in this case, is make your negative thoughts and emotions even more intense than usual, creating a feeling within you that grows more and more intolerable by the minute. Next thing you know, you give in to the urge to act unproductively, and you've sabotaged yourself in the process.

Now, there's a temptation to conclude that your emotions are what get you into trouble. It may be the truth; however, if you judge your emotions as bad, you will be overlooking one very important fact: emotions matter a lot to humanity. For the most part, judgments are often made in a moment and based on highly inaccurate perceptions of the world around you. More often than not, this happens because we need to get to the point as quickly as possible and snap judgments offer a shortcut, so we can save time. The downside to this is if you pass judgment mindlessly, you will find that you're swimming in pain and suffering, and you're back to being buffeted about by your emotions.

Judgments and Emotions

If you're observant, you will have noticed that your thinking is often affected by your mood. In turn, your thinking can and does affect your judgment as well. If you've got BPD, you'll find that your mood is the root cause of your behavior. Your memories and judgments will always be affected by your mood. In other words, if you're feeling glum at the moment and you think about your childhood, chances are the memories that will come to you will be sad ones. But if you're feeling really great, and you think back to your younger days, you'll remember the happy times. In fact, your mood is so powerful it can actually color the very same experience in two completely different ways.

When you make a judgment about anything, you'll find that you become partial to anything that supports your point of view. In other words, you lose all sense of objectivity. You ignore anything that is evidence to the contrary of what you believe to be true. You may have heard the term "confirmation bias." This passive refusal to be objective is exactly what confirmation bias refers to.

When you factor in the fact that BPD patients have to deal with a constant instability in their mood, depression, and anxiety, then this becomes an even bigger problem. The passing judgment doesn't just make you contend with intensely uncomfortable emotions, but you have an even narrower mindset on account of this.

Culturally, we deem emotions like excitement, love, joy, and fun amongst others as being "good" while anger, fear, sadness, guilt, and others are "bad." The trouble is not necessarily the "bad" emotions, but the judgment about them to begin with. While it is true that certain emotions are simply more desirable compared to others, we must begin to think of emotions in a nonjudgmental light. The onus is on us to really observe and notice all that comes up when we experience whatever emotions we feel, without labeling it good or bad. In other words, the skill you need to learn is to label emotions for what they are, and nothing more. Simply noting the way your body feels and the thoughts that go through your mind when you feel emotion is more than enough.

As you mindfully observe your emotions, with no judgment, it will become even clearer to you that emotions actually morph. They never remain the same, and they never stick around. When you realize this, you will become even more comfortable with feeling things, even the "bad," because you know it will pass anyway. So you won't feel the need to suppress the emotions, and you won't be interested in enhancing it either. The result? Anger that lasts about 20 seconds, max. I know, it's incredible! But it is real. It can be your reality too. Speaking of reality, let's move on to the next segment.

Being Okay With What Is

Now that you understand non-judgment, we shall move on to the idea of acceptance. This is about seeing your reality for what it is and accepting it just so, with no judgment whatsoever. You will hear of this as **radical acceptance**, in DBT.

It can be incredibly hard for some people to accept themselves the way they are. They find it hard to be okay with the way their lives are for a variety of reasons. They might think that they've been dealt a very unfair hand, and who in their right mind would want to be okay with that? That is a very fair question to ask.

When you find it in you to be okay with your reality as is, not questioning, fighting, or judging it, then and only then will you be able to see how your world came to be the way it is. You will be able to see the part you played in making things the way you are. You will also have the answer to the question of how you should go about creating the world you prefer.

People have the erroneous idea that once you accept your reality that means you can do nothing about it. They think it means just resigning yourself to your fate, and being okay with the rest of your life being as it is right now. This is not the case. Accepting your reality doesn't mean you should "find a way to love it," or that you should agree with the status quo. All it means is that you see it for what it is. When you do, the way you react to stressful situations will change dramatically for the better. You will be more at ease with yourself, and with what's going on around. From this powerful place of ease and calm, you can then begin to navigate your way to a better life.

Acceptance: Challenge Accepted

Acceptance is no mean feat. You've got to be willing to accept your reality, several times over, because it's very easy to move back into a state of non-acceptance, in a bid to avoid the pain and other strong emotions you will have to deal with when you open your heart and your eyes to your reality.

To practice self-acceptance is an even more difficult thing than accepting the reality of a situation. A lot of people with BPD are constantly very critical of themselves, judging themselves with no mercy. They assume that they are incapable of being loved and that they don't even deserve love in the first place. People with BPD are not particularly great at making positive judgments, so none of this works out well for them in any way. They are perpetually plagued by self-loathing and a refusal to accept themselves as they are. This, of course, leads to a lot of suffering.

In practicing mindfulness, you will find that you cannot run away from acceptance and self-compassion. In fact, there is a rather ancient mediation known as **Metta**, which is also called the **loving-kindness meditation.** Metta teaches you to pay attention to the good in others, rather than the bad stuff that makes others pain to be around. A lot of your suffering is on account of your negative judgments. So if you can flip your attention over to the positive side, you can get rid of the bulk of your suffering. This does not mean you become blind to the bad stuff about other people; it's just that you choose compassion and positivity over everything else, every time. This way, you don't have to suffer from the emotions of disappointment, bitterness, hatred, and dissatisfaction. This also has the added benefit of helping you learn to be nonjudgmental.

Practicing Metta

Sit in a comfortable chair for three minutes. You will repeat a chant or a short phrase, over and over. You can also repeat other phrases, which are just like the original phrase, as long as they are all about giving love and kindness to the people in your life that you want to feel compassionate about and give compassion to or the people you constantly judge negatively. You can also use this on yourself whenever you are critical of yourself. Here are some phrases you can use:

May I be free and safe.

May I be light, and whole.

May I be at ease.

May I be peaceful.

May I be full of joy.

May I be full of loving-kindness.

Try this and check-in with yourself when you're done. How do you feel? Notice that. You can also replace "I" with someone else's name if you're struggling with them, or simply want to send them love and light.

Besides making this a daily practice, you could also try this when you find you're judgmental towards someone or yourself. You can gently and firmly say, *May you be free from suffering.* What you'll find is that the pattern of negativity will be interrupted, as well as the emotions, which usually accompany the negative thoughts.

In order to create lasting change, you will need to build your awareness. This means you become more aware of the choices you make, the emotions you feel, and the things, which trigger you into acting the way, you do. Once you're aware of what motivates your behavior, then you'll be able to do something about it. It should go without saying that being non-judgmental is key, as you become aware of your life. It means you also need to be aware of when you're judgmental, and not judge yourself for being judgy. All you need to do when you notice you've got a judgment that does not serve you is to try labeling it as factually as you can or rephrasing the judgment so that what you have left is a nonjudgmental truth.

Mindfulness Practices to Increase Awareness

Discomfort and Pain

This will take you all of three minutes. First of all, check yourself for parts of your body that are in pain, whether it's tightness in your muscles, a headache, or a sore throat. You want to find that one discomfort that you're the most judgmental about. Once you find it, observe and notice what your thoughts are. Pay attention so you can find the thoughts, which are judgmental. As they come up, simply relabel them so that there is no longer any judgment, and it's all just based on facts.

Politics

For half an hour or a full hour, watch a news station, or you could read the papers if you prefer that. Make sure the paper or station leans a different way than you do politically. As you watch or read, pay attention to the judgmental thoughts that come up. Next, see about relabeling these thoughts so that they are no longer judgmental.

One Thing at a Time

The next skill we're going to address is known in DBT as doing everything "one-mindfully." In other words, no multitasking. If you're walking the dog, you're walking the dog. If you're eating, all you're doing is eating. If you're hanging out with a friend, then no cell phone is distracting you from your friend or the moment. If you're writing, then you're writing, not listening to music **and** writing at the same time.

In today's world, there is much love for multitasking. It is very rare to find someone who's doing just one thing at a time. You're making toast while on the phone while firing off an email while placing a trade while booking a trip while making love to your significant other. It's crazy! But that's the world we're in right now.

When you learn to do one thing at a time, you will find it to be completely empowering. It's also a bit of a challenge since today's world values and over prioritizes the ability to multitask.

The only way to achieve one-mindedness is just to stop trying to do so much at once. In other words, just let go of all the thoughts clamoring for your attention, and focus your mind, body, and soul into just one task at a time, in the present. It may seem like there is no way you could achieve this when you've got deadlines, and you're running late, but it gets easier. At first, when you practice one-mindedness, it will feel like you're a little too slow at whatever it is you're doing. However, the more you practice, the more you will find you're more efficient with your time and energy. You will also see a significant decrease in your stress levels, and you'll become more of a pro at what you're doing. This is old wisdom that our ancestors had always known.

When you do two things at the same time, you might as well be doing nothing.

When you want to practice one-mindedness, devote the whole of your time, energy, and attention to the task at hand. Do this with no judgments, and with no self-consciousness. Just become one with what you're doing, like a method actor becomes his role, whether the cameras are on or not. As you do what you do, with your awareness fully at the moment, you will find your life becomes full of ease and flow. You're in the moment. You're Zen.

Not-So-Fun Facts about Multitasking

When you multitask:

• You're unable to recall whatever it is you're learning while multitasking easily.

• You don't attain the level of success you should because of your scattered focus.

• You are inefficient at your tasks, as you keep switching focus around.

• You are stressed out, which is something you don't need when you have BPD.

- You find it hard to learn new information or skills.

- You only get mediocre results with all that you're doing.

Mindfulness Practices for One Mindedness

Breakfast

As you have your breakfast, just sit and eat. Do nothing else. Do not read a paper or even the back of a cereal box. Notice the way you experience your food. Notice when you feel the urge to do something else as you eat, like check your phone. As your mind wanders, bring it back to the experience of you having breakfast. Focus on the tastes, smells, sights, temperatures, textures, and little things you need to do like spreading butter on toast.

Driving

When you drive, do not put your radio on. Do not make any calls on your phone. Focus on one thing alone: the act of driving. Notice the simple, yet profound movements you make which move the care forwards. Notice the road, the asphalt before you, and the other metal and chrome boxes around you. When you forget to focus, simply return your attention gently and lovingly to all that driving entails.

Television

When you watch TV, put your phone away. Don't check your email. Don't eat a snack. Just focus on whatever is on the television. Nothing else.

Dishes

When you do the dishes, focus on only that. Do not sing or hum. Don't play music. Just focus on the task at hand. Notice the water, the difference when you've got the soap going, the feel of the sponge in your hand. Notice how your plates feel different when clean versus when dirty. When your mind wanders, come back to the dishes, and focus.

Lists

First thing in the morning, create a list of things you plan to accomplish for the day. Make sure you list them in order of importance. You do not get to begin the second task unless and until you are done with the first. If for some reason you are unable to finish with your list that day, simply continue with it the next day, until you're done.

Act In Accordance with the Circumstance

This is the last skill you need to learn when it comes to mindfulness. It's known as "effectiveness." This basically means you do what you need to do at the moment. You don't react from a need to be right, or a need for justice for some slight you perceived against you, but you react the way you do because the situation at hand calls for it. This way, you can save your relationships. Another way you can act in accordance with the situation is when you're in a situation where everyone is eating a new Indian dish with their hands, and you haven't quite worked out how to eat your meal the same way. In that situation, just use a fork like you normally would. Or were you pulled over by the police for going a bit over the speed limit, ***"just like every other driver?"*** Then rather than argue your point because you need to be right, simply do what the moment calls for: Accept the consequence you're faced with. If you don't, the more you argue, the angrier you'll make the cop, and the more likely things will escalate to an undesirable scenario.

Mindfulness Practices for Effectiveness

Past Behavior

Do you recall a time when you were more concerned about being right than simply making a more effective choice? Think about what emotions plagued you at the time. Now, knowing what you know, what do you think you could change about your reaction? How would your preferred reaction have played out? Think about it.

Family

Bring to mind a time there was a family member who was very wrong to have done what they did. Do you think there might have been some benefit if you had simply let go of the whole thing, rather than continue harping on about how you're right?

Chapter Nine: Mindfulness Practices for All Dysregulation

Without much ado, we're going to jump right into all the mindfulness practices, which can help with emotional, interpersonal, behavioral, and cognitive Dysregulation, as well as self-Dysregulation. Let's begin!

Mindfulness Practices for Emotional Dysregulation

These practices are to help you handle your emotions better and to take charge of them, so you do not give in to the urges to act in ways that do not serve you.

Noticing and Labeling

First, observe the sensations in your body. Next, feel out the urges that you have to act. Next, try to suss out the emotion driving these urges. Then do your best to express what you feel as nonjudgmentally as you can. Breathe deeply, keeping your hands and the rest of your body open. Make sure you stay grounded. Now, as you do this, observe your emotion as though it were an ocean wave.

If you're trying to use this during a particularly tasking situation emotionally speaking, then do take some time out before you begin this practice. You can also use noticing and labeling when it comes to contagious emotions. Remember, people with BPD easily pick up on other people's emotions and make them their own. By the simple act of noticing where the emotion is coming from, and then labeling it, you can dissipate that unneeded toxic energy that you feel.

Non-Anger

Whenever you sense you're feeling angry, upset, irritated, or frustrated with someone, first identify the anger that you feel on the inside by noticing the way it shows up in your body. Do this with no judgment. Once you've done that, the next step is to practice acts of non-anger towards the person or situation you're dealing with. You could choose to help them out with work or financially. You could give them a hug, or wish them a lovely day. As you practice non-anger, you will notice the anger you feel reducing, until it no longer exists. Your suffering will then vanish into thin air, and you'll have found a better way to deal with conflicts.

Mindfulness Practices for Interpersonal Dysregulation

These practices help you in building, restoring, and saving your interpersonal relationships.

Becoming Stable

The whole point behind this practice is to show you how your mood affects your perception of others and to help you realize that the relationships you have with others matter more than the very fleeting emotion you're dealing with at the moment. You will be better off doing this with a curious mind.

First, you would need to become aware of your attitude and your customary reactions. So whenever you are feeling calm, take time to really think about at least five people who are near and dear to you. Think of those relationships, which happen to depend on your mood alone.

Next, think of all the times you were struck by particular emotions, and consider whether or not those emotions actually affected your feelings for these people. Once you've done that, it's time for noticing and labeling. Go through all the emotions and judgments you assigned to each person. As you do this, you will find you're becoming even more aware and better at realizing how your mood affects your relationships.

Over time, you should find that as you continue paying attention, you will be even more mindful from moment to moment, especially when your mood at the time is urging you to act unproductively. Ideally, you want to apply this exercise to memories of times you were terrified, sad, in love or loving, excited, bored, and angry. Cover that whole range of emotions. Journal what you notice, and go through your journal to see if you can find common threads or keys to unlock a deeper understanding of yourself.

Usual Responses

We all have various ways of responding to different situations in our lives. This exercise will help you become more aware of what your habits are when it comes to your responses. It is important that you take some time out to really consider the answers to these questions. Again, do not be judgmental about any of this. Be like the detached scientist who is gathering data, and nothing more. Be neutral, or at the very least, go easy on yourself. This is not an indictment.

How do you react in your troublesome relationships?
Do you find that you tend to begin arguments, or escalate them whenever you're feeling angry? DO you break stuff, or just seethe and sulk in silence? Do you shut down or lash out? Do you harass the other person with lots and lots of texts? Are you more withdrawn? Is your anger passive-aggressive? Do you simply wall yourself off, refusing to be a part of activities

involving your friends because you're upset with one or all of them?

What is your habit of thought in your troublesome relationships? When you are angry, do you think about how terrible the other person is? Do you have fearful thoughts about how they are going to leave you for good this time? Do you think to yourself that you're an awful individual, always starting up some sort of trouble? Do you find yourself thinking that you're impossible to love?

Act and Think

It's easy to do your mindful practices when you're in a calm state of mind, but what happens when you are the furthest thing from calm? Besides, the trouble in your relationship never happens when you are in a state of ease anyway. The whole point behind asking you to do these practices when you are calm is kind of like why we have fire drills. Once you've practiced and practiced, when a real-life situation calls for one of these skills, you're able to draw on it easily, because it's become second nature to you. When you're calm, it's easier to identify when you're starting to fall apart, than when you're right in the heart of things.

However, let's talk about what you're going to do when you find yourself in the heat of the moment. There are two things that can put your relationships at risk: your actions and your thoughts. So as you practice being mindful, you will find that you're better at handling things as they come up at the moment. You will no longer feel like you're being ambushed.

So here is how to act mindfully at the moment. First, take a deep breath. Keep breathing deep, and remain grounded in what's happening right now. As emotions arise, and they will just label them as nonjudgmentally as you can. Listen very closely to what the other party is telling you, and beware of any temptation you have to judge or to twist their words to suit your perceptions. Next, if you are actually at fault, then do not be shy about apologizing. Having done that express willingly that you understand, you both have different perspectives on things. Finally, be open by doing your best to consider all the various parts of your relationship. Be determined to stay open to all things, be they positive, neutral, or negative.

If you find that your thoughts are less than constructive, then here's the part of the exercise focused on how to think productively: first things first, take a deep breath and just slow down a bit. Keep your hands open, and your palms turned upwards. Then take a moment to think about whether or not you're misinterpreting the situation in your head. Next, remember that your thoughts are not you, and they are not the truth either. Finally, do be kind to yourself.

Becoming an Open Book

As someone with BPD, more often than not, you find yourself feeling misunderstood. Whenever you feel this way, here's what you can do: first, ground yourself by focusing on your breath. Take long, slow breaths, so you can calm down and be in the moment. Next, let it be known that you would like some space so you can sort out the way that you're feeling in the moment, and deal with being misunderstood. Next, really think about the other options that exist, besides the one you're so besotted with when it comes to the other person's stance. When you're done, keep your temper even by recalling that at the end of the day, everyone is doing as well as they can. Then go back and express your side as best as you can, while also accepting that the other person's point of view is just as valid as yours is.

Mindfulness Practices for Behavioral Dysregulation

These practices are to help you get a better grip on your urges, and the choices you settle on when you do act out based on your emotions.

Meeting Your Demons

This is useful if you find yourself struggling with suicidal thoughts, or you've made an actual attempt, or you constantly self-harm. Step one is noticing and labeling the state of mind you are in at the moment. Are you coming from a state of "not good enough," "suicidal" or "self-harming"? Then the next thing you want to do is ask yourself, "Is this thought process of any use at all right now?" Answer a straight yes, or no. This is the one time when you should be black-and-white about anything. If you answered yes, then the next thing you need to do is let go, and just observe the thoughts like a third party, with disinterest, keeping in mind that if you keep wrestling the thoughts to the ground, they will beat you up eventually, and things will get ugly. If you answered no, then you need to think of other places you can direct your attention to. You could recall something you found extremely calming in the past, or you could recall something that was fun or felt good. Just imagine your mind is an object you can pick up and move about, like moving it from AngerVille to Happy Meadows. When you find your mind wandering back to the unproductive thought triggering your undesirable emotions — and it will happen — just pick your mind up again and move back to Happy Meadows, or do something that requires you to be logical, like a crossword puzzle or Sudoku or something. This is a practice you need to keep working on, but soon, you'll find it incredibly beneficial.

Mindfulness Practice for Impulsiveness

For this one, you need to sit in a mindful position. You will also need to get a timer going for about half a minute to two minutes. What you need to do is observe the urge you feel to swallow. Notice as the saliva gathers in your mouth, begging you to swallow already. Notice what happens in your mind, and notice how you start to feel agitated. Drool if you must, but you must not swallow. Do not give in to the urge until your timer goes off. Observe as the urge builds in intensity, but just sit, calmly, and do nothing. Once you've done this, you can swallow.

Immovable

Make sure that you're all alone for this one. Now make a promise to yourself that whenever next you notice the urge to give in to self-destructive behavior, you will do this practice instead. You may lie on the floor if you want to, or you could sit in a chair instead. A floor is a great option because you will find it literally grounding. The task is simple but not easy. You will remain in that position without moving, no matter how badly you want to get up. You will not move until the urge you feel has tapered off and then is gone for good. There is no time for this exercise, and for a good reason. The urge gong away is all the timer you need. As you remain seated or remain on the floor, do pay attention to your breath. Also, make full use of your noticing and labeling skills when it comes to your thoughts and emotions. What you will find is that shockingly, you can actually wait out the impulsive urges that previously had you in their grip.

Mindfulness Practices for Cognitive Dysregulation

These practices are particularly helpful for when you can feel a dissociative episode coming on, or some other form of cognitive Dysregulation.

The Ice Challenge

Whenever you're feeling floaty and dissociated, try this on for size: Get a bowl and fill it with ice water. Then just dunk your whole face into the bowl, and keep it there. As your face remains in the icy cold water, focus on the temperature of the water. Focus on the way it feels on your skin. A good side effect of this practice is that it will activate your dive reflex, which means your breathing and heart rate will slow down, making your physiology calmer. This is a useful practice to do when you've got a panic attack, or you can feel one coming on.

Yet another exercise you could try is to listen to really loud music, smell something with a strong, sharp scent, or bite into something sour like a lemon, or pop a teaspoon full of salt into your mouth — but please do NOT swallow. Anything that requires really activating your physical senses is great to snap you back to the present moment and keep you grounded.

Getting a Mindful Kit

If you find that you're always troubled by episodes of dissociation, then it would help to carry a kit around with you, which helps you stay grounded and at the moment. To figure out what would be in your kit, you need to know what it is you have a very strong, visceral reaction to, so you can put it in there.

For taste, you could use strongly flavored pieces of gum. The best way to go is cinnamon or a very strong mind. You could also opt for sour sweets, which are sure to bring you back. Be sure to really focus on the taste as best as you can.

For sensation, all you need is something that's either hot or cold. Yom could use ice cubes if you can get access to them. Just hold them in your hand till they melt away. Another thing you could do is suck on the ice cubes, or you could stand on them, or put them on a sensitive body part such as the inside of your wrists, or the back of your ears. You could also just run some cold water over your hands, or splash some on your face.

For smell, all you need is a scent that's strong enough. If the scent triggers a memory with strong emotions attached, then that's even better. If you can't think of a scent that would do that, that's okay. Just try out different ones to see what does the trick for you. A lot of people report that sharp, crisp scents help them a lot. You could also opt for your significant other's favorite perfume as well. Try dryer sheets too, as people have good things to say about them.

For sight, you could choose a shape that stands out to you, or color, a number, or even a letter. Look around and look for your preferred object whenever you've got a case of the runaways, and that should help you stay grounded. If you chose a color, say yellow, you can begin looking for the color around you, and as you do, run a little monologue in your head that goes something like, "I see a man with a yellow handkerchief, a child playing with a yellow ball, a yellow taxi driving past..." Do this for about ten minutes, or until you feel yourself becoming more grounded in the here and now.

When it comes to sounds, all you need is music that you love. Make a whole playlist of those songs, which ground you, and keep them handy on your phone or mp3 player.

Finally, when it comes to touch, all you need to do is feel different textures with your hands. Feel the fabric of your clothes, or the textures of the paint on the walls, or the table. Whatever it convenient and handy. Pay attention to the difference in textures. Use various parts of your body to feel various objects.

Non-Judgment and Objectiveness

When you're dealing with paranoia, you'll find this practice helpful. This works if you catch the paranoid thoughts coming on early. All you have to do is label the thoughts as "my paranoid thoughts." This already communicates to you that these thoughts should not be taken seriously. Next, find a quiet spot and pay attention to your breath. When you feel your emotions coming on, make use of your grounding kit to remain centered. The thoughts are just thoughts, so do not be judgmental about them. Now ask yourself what the facts are right here and now. What evidence have you got to support any of these paranoid thoughts? Then remind yourself as gently as you can that you don't have to buy into all of your thoughts. Do this as you keep breathing. Net, try to think of other alternatives to your paranoid thoughts.

Mindfulness Practices for Self-Dysregulation

These practices are the best for when you feel like you're starting to lose touch with yourself.

Noticing and Labeling Your Changes

People with BPD often find that they assume role after role, never being aware in the moment. Mindfulness can fix this because it helps you expand your awareness. For this practice, all you need to do is take time out to create a list of all the changes you have undergone. The goal is not to keep score against yourself, but to notice, with no judgment, all the ways you have changed. Become curious about yourself. Once you are done with the list, then you only have to pay attention for a week to how you change each day and add this to your list as well. As you update your list, you will begin to notice a pattern emerge, in the changes you go through. Take your time to really think about these changes. Just notice and label them. Don't do anything more. Next, you will need to do some soul searching.

How often do your goals change? How often have you begun tasks with the aim of achieving your goal, only to give up and do something entirely different? Is this something that happens repeatedly? Do you find that your goals are very much affected by what the people around you think or by your mod at the moment? What are the triggers that cause you to abandon your old goals for new ones?

As for your values and attitudes, do you find that they're always changing? Reflect on the times you've committed to a goal or a decision, and you chose to act in a way that made you feel uncomfortable or even surprised you. Do you find that your values change depending on who you're with at the moment?

Now, let's do some self-evaluation when it comes to your identity. Do you take on different identities from one situation to another? Do you change the way you speak or the way you dress? How would all the different people in your life describe you as a person? Would they have different ideas of you, or would their descriptions match one another's for the most part?

Finding Your Breath

You will have noticed by this point how important the breath is when it comes to mindfulness. It helps you stay centered, grounded, and in your own flesh. The great thing about the breath is you can always return to it wherever you are, no matter what you're dealing with at the moment.

Go someplace quiet and sit down mindfully. What you will be doing in this practice is simply counting your breaths. You could use numbers, or you could count with an image in your head such as stairs, an elevator going up or down, or a ladder. You're going to do this for two minutes at a go for starters, and if you feel like increasing the time limit later, you can do that, too. Each count will cover both your inhale and your exhale. In other words, as you breathe in, and then out, that's one count. When you breathe in, and then out again, that's count number two, and so on and so forth. When you count, do not try to make your breath match the counting. Rather, let the counting match your natural pattern of breathing. You might find the pacing to be a bit odd, but that's fine, as long as you're comfortable. When your mind wanders off, as usual, be gentle as you bring it back, and begin again at one. No matter how many times you have to start from one, never beat yourself up. It's good that you're noticing your mind wandering. Over time, it will wander less and less. In fact, the goal of this practice is not about hitting high numbers, but about noticing when your mind wanders and deliberately bringing it back.

The way this benefits you is that it helps you remain in the moment, and helps you experience whatever is going on right now without reacting in any way. Also, the more you practice this, the more you will find your intuition is spot on about things. Your intuition is the whole reason you're able to find a connection to the things that matter the most to you. This exercise is a great way to slow down your reaction to things, as well.

Chapter Ten: Releasing Negative Thoughts

Mindfulness is the ultimate key to help you release the negative thoughts, which make you suffer. For the most part, people turn to all sorts of distractions or seek out the bottle or some drug to make them feel better. These only work in the short term. Eventually, they wind up, regretting their choices. Perhaps you've been here too, yourself. It's a real struggle, and it isn't easy to just get rid of negative thoughts. However, mindfulness can be your secret weapon.

In all situations, you must first become aware, if you're going to rid yourself of negativity. When you become aware, you can even go a step further and be proactive about making your brain more positive, by training it to think positively, the same way you taught it to think negatively — by repetition. Remember, this is how you build a habit.

The First Step: Recognition

You need to be able to recognize the negative habits of thought. You'll find that they are incredibly unhelpful and frequently leave you in a state of mind that drains you. You feel anxious, depressed, sad, angry, frustrated, and just sick of it all. You're full of fear that it's never going to end, and you've got the burden of shame because you feel there is something terribly wrong with you, and everyone else is judging you for it.

The good news is once you recognize negative thoughts as they happen, you can do something about them. You can take a step back from them, reminding yourself as often as you need to that thoughts are only thoughts, and they are no facts. In fact, go a step further and accept that some of your thoughts are flat out lies. Don't judge yourself for having these thoughts; they are not you. They are simply the end result of a brain that's working. As you step back even further from your thoughts (cognitive diffusion), you get to notice that thoughts are not reality. You don't need to buy into them. You do not need to take them too seriously. If you do, then you will find yourself sucked into a negative pattern of thinking again.

The Second Step: Returning to Your Senses

For the most part, negative thoughts either come from past regrets or issues and fears of the future. You hardly ever get negative thoughts that are about the present. It might seem like your negative thought is about the situation at hand, but more often than not, if you dig beneath the surface, you will find that the thoughts are rooted in your past or your future and not the now. So the solution becomes evident: You must become present. To be present means you are completely aware of the facts as they are right now, with no extraneous explanation or justification or analysis. We've already talked about various practices you can use to ground yourself in the present, in previous chapters.

The Third Step: Consistent Mindfulness

You've got to stay consistent with your practice, so you can build two new habits: Stopping negative thinking in its tracks, and replacing it with positive, empowering thoughts. It is consistency, which will give you results. You don't get to be mindful today, and mindless tomorrow. You don't say, "Okay, I had a fair bit of oxygen today, so tomorrow I'm just not going to breathe." You keep going. Soon, it becomes second nature, and you'll see the benefits in your life.

The Fourth Step: Ask the Right Questions

If you find it hard to release negative thoughts by observing and labeling, then you can simply ask yourself: Are these thoughts useful or of help to me? Are they true, beyond the shadow of a doubt? Could they just be a rerun of an old episode my mind loves to play as a habit? Are these thoughts helping me take action that is effective? Are these thoughts helpful, or is my mind simply making noise? Then you can go a step further by asking yourself constructive questions like these: What is the truth I hold dear? What is it that I really want to make of this situation, and how can I make it happen? How can I do my best with the state of things right now? What is a new, better idea that I can direct my attention to right now? Is there any way I can look at this differently? Is there something I can appreciate about the moment? These questions will help you turn your attention from the negative to the positive. You will be more focused on all that is going right in your life. As a result, you will have a life that is richer than ever, a life that you fall deeper and deeper in love with every day.

Conclusion

So we've come to the end of this book. I want you to know that life with BPD is not the end of the world. You do not need to resign yourself to suffering. You do not need to resign yourself to misery, and you don't have to put up with any of it for one moment longer. In this book, you have the keys you need to break free of the chains that you've worn on your neck for most of your life.

There will be times when you feel like it's impossible to keep going but just think: You've read this book. That's step one. You can't quit now. There's no looking back. You are now well on your way to a mindful life.

As you practice living mindfully, you will notice your life becoming more magical. You will feel your heart soaring. You will sense a burden being lifted from your soul as you continue to grow in awareness, presence, and mindfulness. You will notice all the patterns that you've been blind to before now, and you'll find that as you notice them, you're able to let them go.

One day, sooner than you think, you will look back, and you will find that you have become an entirely different person. You will have become new. You, too, will become a source of hope for thousands out there who are struggling with BPD as you once did. You will be one more living proof that mindfulness can indeed help you become who you're really supposed to be.

As you practice, you'll find that beliefs you have held for the longest time will be tested. You will find it so hard to let go of mindsets you've treasured for so long, sometimes. When this happens, I want you to think about how far you've come. I want you to think about all that you stand to gain, and ask yourself if holding on to your former paradigms is worth losing a chance to live a life you've only ever dreamed of. I'm going to assume your answer to that is a loud and resounding no. So get back at it, each and every time.

Just like you never beat up on yourself when your attention wanders during mindfulness practice, do not beat up on yourself if you find you've taken a break or fallen off the wagon. In fact, moments like that are a gift because they give you the opportunity to practice self-compassion and self-forgiveness. So with gentle, loving-kindness, get back to your journey of mindfulness, as often as you need to. Soon, it will become second nature.

You've got to make a decision to commit to this. Stay curious. Always be willing to learn. Always be willing to push past your comfort zone. This is how you grow.

Do this for yourself. You deserve it, don't you think?

I believe you do. I believe in you.

Manufactured by Amazon.ca
Bolton, ON